toys to grow with

toys to grow with

John J. Fisher

Hundreds of Play Ideas
For Babies and Toddlers

COLLINS

First published in this edition in 1988 by
William Collins Sons & Co. Ltd
London · Glasgow · Sydney
Auckland · Johannesburg

Published in the United States in 1986 by
The Putnam Publishing Group

Photographs by Bill Parsons,
courtesy of Johnson & Johnson Child Development Products
Illustrations by Sandra Pond
Cover photograph by Fiona Pragoff

British Library Cataloguing in Publication Data
Fisher, John J.
    Toys to grow with.
    1. Toys. Making – Manuals – For children
    I. Title
    745.592

ISBN 0 00 412387 5

Set in Garamond
by Ace Filmsetting Ltd, Frome
Printed and bound in Great Britain
by Hartnolls Ltd, Bodmin

Contents

homemade toys: by ideal introduction age

read this first 1

The more that child development specialists study the early years, the more they value young children's experiences; experiences that we can call play. Play is how a young child practises — and consequently perfects — emerging physical, mental, social and language skills. Since development and learning are cumulative, early experiences are the foundation of nearly all future skills.

This isn't news to today's parents and teachers. You *know* that play is as important as it is fun. Yet, with so many responsibilities, so much to think about when bringing up a young child, it's not easy to be a play wizard, whether this is your first baby or your fourth. As a mother exclaimed, 'I know *why* play is so valuable. I need ideas of *what* to do!'

This book is filled with ideas:

- What commercial and homemade toys are good for each age — and how to use them to enjoy and enhance all areas of your child's emerging skills.

- What games other parents (and experts) have found especially valuable at each stage of development.

- What to do when you've exhausted your own bank of favourite play ideas or are just too exhausted to conjure up amazing new delights for your youngest family member.

And yes, there are illuminating discussions of *why* certain activities are so beneficial, too.

These play ideas and homemade toys come from years of research, both in libraries and in all kinds of daily environments: child care centres, special play labs and, most importantly, homes. As co-creator of the Johnson & Johnson Child Development Toys in the United

States, I've been lucky to work closely with hundreds of families and scores of teachers. I hope this book helps you enjoy your child's first three years, and makes learning through play even more fun for the whole family.

—————— DO BABIES NEED TOYS? ——————

Let's face it straight away: **Do babies need toys?**

Yes.

Throughout the early years, your child develops all kinds of skills, from hit-or-miss batting to reaching with sure co-ordination to understanding spatial relationships. Objects play a vital part.

For instance, consider physical skills, like reaching and grasping, using both hands simultaneously, or throwing with accuracy. To master these and scores of other skills, a baby needs to practise them over and over again. Obviously, he needs objects with which to practise, objects that are safe and easy for him to handle.

Toys build intellectual skills, too. Young children learn best through direct experiences with the world around them. In a sense, they work things out with their hands before their heads – and the former leads directly to the latter. By handling toys, stacking them into towers, knocking them down, fitting one toy over or into another, hiding and finding them, lining them up, counting them – in short, experimenting with all the ways parts can be related to one another – a young child learns concepts such as size, shape, space, number, and so on. Toys can enhance language, social and emotional skills as well, as you'll see throughout this book. Yes, babies do need toys.

But remember – this book considers a toy to be *any* object that your child plays with:

o Playthings you buy (there are some excellent ones on the market).

o Toys you make at home (there are plenty of those in this book).

o Household objects from the kitchen, the scrapbox, the throw-away pile.

And remember, too, that toys are most successful when matched to your child's particular age or developmental stage. Toys that are too

sophisticated will baffle or frustrate him (or, even worse, be dangerous); those that are too simple will bore. Your baby's play needs change
as his interests and skills develop, so you need to decide when to
introduce appropriate toys and games. There are guidelines throughout this book.

MAKING YOUR OWN TOYS

Among the scores of play ideas in this book are about fifty toys you can
make. Every one meets some very basic standards:

○ All help your young child develop important skills.

○ All have been tested with parents and children.

○ All are made from common or easily obtained materials. In fact, most
of these playthings can be made from a handful or two of indispensable
items described in Homemade Toys: Invaluable Materials (page 186).

○ Each serves a primary purpose that is not duplicated by a toy that you
can buy. On the other hand, there are several well-designed commercial toys that are safer and more durable than anything you could hope
to create without sophisticated machines and materials. Both serve an
important purpose in your child's development.

○ Since parents and teachers are so busy, all are simple to create. In fact,
each toy can be made in about thirty minutes – or less.

SAFETY ESSENTIALS

Toys you make probably aren't going to be as safe as most of those you
buy. Also, many homemade toys and household items are wonderful
for supervised play, but might become dangerous should a child use
them without your watchful eye. All the homemade toys included here
have been devised with safety in mind. Please heed the warning if a toy
is indicated FOR SUPERVISED PLAY ONLY. You'll also find all kinds of
SAFETY NOTES throughout this book; some of these are general,
whereas some are related to specific playthings (commercial as well as
homemade). It's a good idea to read them.

Play is fun but it also encourages valuable learning skills.

—— HOW THIS BOOK IS ORGANIZED——

These games and toys are organized into general skill areas: Early Eye-catchers (visual stimulation for a very young baby), Activities for Hands (and Heads), Active Play and Exercise, and the like. Some categories are sub-divided, too, where appropriate. Bear in mind that such divisions are arbitrary and by no means restrictive. Almost every toy, every game, enhances more than a single skill, no matter how broad the category.

The toys and games within a category (and sometimes sub-category) are generally listed chronologically by the child's age. Nearly all suggest the appropriate introductory age as well. This is also some-what arbitrary – every baby is different, grows and learns at his own rate, and has an individual pattern of development.

And lastly, each homemade toy has specific age guidelines:

○ The *ideal intro age* is the age at which most children begin using the toy for its primary purpose – be it batting or handling or climbing or fantasy play.

○ The *age range* is the total stretch of time most children will enjoy the toy.

Sometimes the age range begins before the ideal age of introduction. For example, although many children enjoy some facets of the Toddler Trampoline starting at 15 months (or even younger), it's at 18 months that this toy really comes into its own.

These age guidelines are based mostly on children's typical behaviour, sometimes on safety considerations. To repeat: *they are only guidelines.* Since your child is unique, he may enjoy an activity before or after the age given. You know your child best and can adapt the ages.

NOTE: For quick reference to all the homemade toys by *ideal intro age* and *age range*, see the list on pages 7–10.

—————— NOTES AND REMINDERS ——————

1. If you have older children as well as a baby or toddler, invite them to join in activities. They might help you make some of these toys, too. Seeing (and helping) their younger brother or sister enjoy a toy they have created can alleviate a lot of jealous feelings.

2. Get together with a friend or two for a toy-making session. And swap projects. You might be a sewing wizard, your friend a graphics genius.

3. So much of how your child enjoys a particular game or toy depends on your own enthusiasm. The exuberant parent truly *can* make a silk purse out of a sow's ear.

4. Not every young child will enjoy every game or toy in this book. After all, each of us has personal preferences. That's one reason why I've included so many ideas. (I certainly don't expect anyone to play all these games!) Try anything that strikes your fancy, but don't force it if your child is unenthusiastic. And if he snubs that dazzling toy you've made today, try it again later on. Or pass it on to another child.

5. He? She? Which pronoun to use? The familiar complaint. Yet there is still no genderless reference. Since children do come in two sexes, half these chapters call the child 'he', the other half 'she'.

6. The symbol ▶, which sometimes appears beside the boxes giving details of how to make homemade toys and games, indicates that instructions are continued on the following page.

early eye-catchers 2

VISUAL PLAY FOR THE
FIRST MONTHS

Most experts who study newborns agree that a baby is eager to learn and play right from birth. But with limited physical skills, she isn't able to explore actively. She cannot yet control her arm and hand movements, for instance, so she's unable to reach for and handle objects skilfully. Nor can she crawl or walk to get those things that interest her. In a wry way, she embodies (and re-interprets) the old quotation 'The spirit is willing but the flesh is weak'. Therefore, a tiny baby explores her new world most actively with her eyes.

Much early play is visual. In fact, even in the delivery room a baby will stare at faces or a picture of a face, and will follow such a picture when it is moved slowly past her eyes. In addition, researchers have found that young babies like to look at simple shapes and patterns that contrast sharply against a background colour. A black and white draughtboard, a distinct face on a stuffed toy, or even a simple brilliant red circle on a light-coloured field catches their eye.

Even though babies can see from birth, their vision isn't perfect. Based on numerous studies, it's believed that newborns focus best on objects about 20 cm to 30 cm (8 in to 12 in) from their eyes. Those closer or further away, though still visible, are blurred. Since your very young baby isn't able to bring things within her range of vision by herself, she depends on you to perk up her immediate surroundings.

Homemade Eye Targets entertain your baby from the earliest weeks.

—— HOMEMADE VISUAL DELIGHTS ——

One way to make your baby's world more exciting is to place bright, simple pictures wherever she may be: cradle, pram or changing table.

Bear in mind that even very young babies like variety, so make several visual delights, and change them often.

HINT: Looking at an eye-catcher, especially a face, can sometimes even calm a restless baby, unless she's hungry or uncomfortable.

EYE TARGETS

Colourful patterned discs to hang from the cotside.
Ideal Intro Age: Birth
Age Range: Birth to 3 months

Tools and Materials

☆ Uncoated white paper plates

☆ Felt-tipped markers; use non-toxic ones, just in case your baby should ever chew on these toys

☆ Ribbon

☆ Single hole punch or scissors

▶

Instructions

1. Draw a bold, simple design on each side of each plate. Good ideas include:

- A bull's-eye
- Squares
- Giant polka dots
- Broad stripes
- Stars
- Simple flowers
- Faces; these are by far the most popular, so make several

2. Punch a hole in the top of each plate and hang it on the side of the cot or pram with a short piece of ribbon. The bottom of the plate should just about touch the mattress.

HINT: You can buy decorated plates at stationers and newsagents which sell party supplies. Choose simple patterns.

SAFETY NOTE: Remove any paper toys from the cot or pram when your baby begins reaching for them — usually between 2 and 3 months. The paper is unsafe for her to chew on.

SHADOWBOX PICTURES

If your baby receives presents of clothing that come in small, flat boxes, use the boxes and the paper they're wrapped in to make dazzling watchables.
Ideal Intro Age: Birth
Age Range: Birth to 3 months

Tools and Materials

☆ Small, shallow gift box

☆ Wrapping paper with bold patterns

☆ Clear adhesive tape

☆ Ribbon

☆ Single hole punch or scissors

Instructions

1. Cover the box top in paper. (To make two Shadowbox Pictures, cover the bottom, separately, as well.) Completely cover the face and four narrow sides, securing the ends of the paper on the underside.

2. Punch a hole in one long, narrow side. Thread a very short piece of ribbon through the hole, making a strong knot on the inside end, and hang the box in the cot or pram as shown. The bottom of the toy should just about touch the cot mattress.

SAFETY NOTE: Remove any paper toys from the cot when your baby begins reaching for them – usually between 2 and 3 months. The paper is unsafe for her to chew on.

PICTURE PARADE

Stand-alone pictures for cot, pram, changing table or playpen (if you start using one early). This is also a terrific concertina book for the older baby.

Ideal Intro Age: Birth

Age Range: Birth to 3 months when baby plays alone; birth to 12 months in supervised play

Tools and Materials

☆ 3 sheets of thin cardboard, each about 20 × 25 cm (8 × 10 in), although the dimensions aren't critical

☆ Old magazines with plenty of full-page colour photographs or advertisements

☆ All-purpose household glue (non-toxic)

☆ Clear adhesive tape, at least 2.5 cm (1 in) wide

☆ Clear Con-Tact paper (self-stick plastic film) (optional)

☆ Scissors

Instructions

1. Cut out six large pictures the same size as the cardboard sheets. Glue a picture to each side of each sheet.

HINT: Let your baby help you choose the pictures to include. Look through magazines together, and use those things that really catch her eye.

2. Lay the sheets side by side, about 3 mm ($\frac{1}{8}$ in) apart. This gap will become a hinge that lets you fold up the finished toy. Tape the sheets together to make a panel of three pictures.

3. Turn the panel over and run a second piece of tape over each gap to complete the hinge.
4. For added durability, completely cover each side with clear Con-Tact paper.

SAFETY NOTE: This toy could be dangerous for the unsupervised baby over 3 months. She might suck or chew off a corner and choke on it.

The Picture Parade perks up the cot or changing table.

Play Tips

Your baby will also like looking at these homemade eye toys when lying on your lap or any flat surface, or, even later, when sitting in her baby seat. (Obviously, you'll have to hold them up for her to see.)

Talk about the objects in the pictures – their colours and shapes, the features of the faces and their happy expressions, the stars just like those in the sky at night – whatever you can think of to describe them. Your baby won't understand all these words, naturally, but she loves listening to your voice. She'll gradually begin to take in what she's hearing.

All these toys for the eyes take on added interest if they move. With your baby lying on her back, s-l-o-w-l-y move a watchable back and forth in front of her eyes. She probably *tracks* its movements (follows the toy with her eyes, as if she's watching a tiny tennis match). From about 2 months or so, she moves her head as well to keep the toy in view.

You can play tracking games with any toy that has bright colours and eye-catching patterns; or put on a bright glove and move your hand for her to track (wiggle your fingers, too); or let her track your face.

CHANGING-TIME WATCHABLES

Parents often ask me, 'What can I do to keep my baby happily occupied while I'm changing her nappy?' I'm not sure whether this question is prompted because they seek new play opportunities, or because they need to keep their baby busy so they can get on with the business at hand. Either way, here are some homemade toy ideas that fill the bill:

○ Changing-table Display.

○ Changing-time Mobile.

HINT: The homemade Picture Parade is ideal for the changing-table, too.

SAFETY NOTE: *Never* leave your baby alone on the changing surface, no matter how young she may be. In the moment you've gone to answer the door or the phone, she might wriggle off.

CHANGING-TABLE DISPLAY

A changeable display for nappy-changing time.
Ideal Intro Age: Birth
Age Range: Birth to 12 months

Tools and Materials

☆ Concertina-type wall rack, with several protruding pegs

☆ Eye-appealing toys: Eye Targets, Shadowbox Pictures, brightly decorated small shopping bags (folded flat), small stuffed animal, rattle, etc.

Instructions

Mount the rack on the wall next to where you usually change your baby, and hang eye toys from the hooks.

COT MOBILES

Nearly everyone buys a cot mobile, the most traditional eye-catcher for the early months. In fact, a recent survey in the United States reported that over 90 per cent of American babies had one. This statistic has not passed the toy industry by, and many mobiles available today (unlike those a few years ago) are well designed.

The appeal of the best mobiles is simple: the eye-catching visual toys rotate slowly while music plays. Since you'd be hard pressed to make one that functions as well, consider buying one. And look for the following features:

o Music. Your baby will enjoy this feature right from birth. In fact, the appealing tinkly music-box sound will soothe her during mildly restless bouts. The visuals will be less important at first until she tends to look up rather than off to the side when lying on her back – usually starting at around 6 weeks.

CHANGING-TIME MOBILE

This special mobile is good once your baby starts looking up, rather than off to the side, when lying on her back (usually around 6 weeks). The arms swing horizontally, so you can position toys right where your baby is looking at the moment.

Ideal Intro Age: 6 weeks
Age Range: 6 weeks to 6 months

Tools and Materials

☆ Fold-away towel rack with at least three arms

☆ Ribbon

☆ Objects to catch the baby's eye:

○ Fancy bows from gift boxes

○ Small toys

○ Small Eye Targets (decorated dessert-sized paper plates: punch a hole through the centre of each plate and hang them so they face down towards your baby)

○ Small disposable aluminium pie plates, suspended like the Eye Targets

Instructions

Mount the rack on the wall next to where you usually change your baby. Make sure it is high enough above the changing surface – about 76 cm (30 in) – so that it won't interfere with changing either now or later, when your baby is more active. Use pieces of ribbon to hang colourful, eye-catching toys from the arms. Remember: for the early months, it's best if the toys hang about 20–30 cm (8–12 in) from her eyes. However, if she can reach up and grab them at this distance, raise them slightly. These are objects to look at, not handle.

HINT: When your baby *can* grab objects dangling above her (usually starting at around 3 or 4 months), replace these watchables with grabbables: rattles, squeaky toys, favourite hand toys, and so on. Hang them from thick elastic, so that when your baby tugs them she doesn't loosen the rack from the wall.

o The music box should play ten minutes or longer on a single winding, otherwise you'll need to wind it frequently, and the scratchy sound this makes is *not* music to your baby's ears. Try to choose a tune that won't drive you mad after hearing it constantly for the first week!

o Visuals should face downwards, towards the baby. If you can reverse them — added interest! — so much the better.

o The support arm should swing sideways, out of the way; this makes it easier to change the cot sheets.

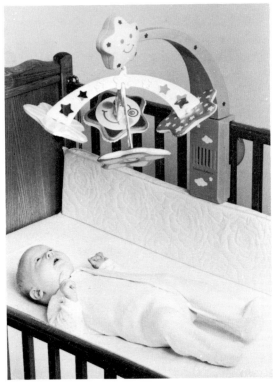

You'll probably want to buy a cot mobile for your baby; check out the guidelines in this chapter for choosing a good one.

SAFETY NOTE: You should probably remove a mobile from the cot when your baby can sit or pull herself to standing (usually between 5 and 6 months). Otherwise she'll probably rip it down — and most mobiles are *not* safe for a baby to handle.

HINT: Once you've removed the mobile, hang a colourful kite on the ceiling. It'll catch the baby's eye and will move delightfully in a breeze. Make sure you attach it securely to a hook or other anchor in the ceiling — it might be dangerous if it fell into the cot.

'SEEING GAMES' FOR LATER MONTHS

Even though your baby starts life nearsighted, she develops almost normal eyesight in a fairly short time. By about 2 or 3 months, she can focus on objects anywhere from a few centimetres to several metres away; and by about 6 months, a baby can focus at various distances nearly as well as an adult with normal vision. Whatever her age, though, she'll continue to enjoy eye games — such as these:

From about 2 months: When she's lying on her back, let her track a toy all the way from one side of her head to the other.

From about 3 months: Lay your baby on her stomach. Dangle a toy in front of her face, then raise it slowly into the air. As she pushes up on her arms to keep the toy in view, she also exercises her arm and back muscles.

From about 2 months, your baby likes to follow toys that move slowly past her face.

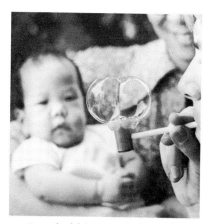

Soap bubbles catch the older baby's eye.

From about 4 to 6 months: You know how popular special effects are in films, so create some for your baby:

o Let her watch you blow soap bubbles.

o Hang a prism in the nursery window. On sunny days it will make rainbows on the wall.

o Wiggle your fingers in front of a torch to make shadow pictures on the wall of the darkened nursery. Or use the torch to pick out different objects in the room, such as pictures on the wall.

o On a sunny day, sit together beneath a window. Make shadow pictures on the floor.

TO SUM UP

Even though eyes are probably your very young baby's best tools for exploring and playing, she's ready for lots of other activities as well. In the next chapter you'll find toys and things for busy hands (and heads).

activities 3 for hands (and heads)

Most psychologists call the first eighteen or so months of life the *sensorimotor period*. This is the time your young child actively explores objects with his five senses: sight, hearing, smell, taste and touch. And does he explore! One researcher, Allison Clarke-Stewart, found that the 9- to 18-month-olds she observed in their homes spent nearly 50 per cent of their waking hours looking at and playing with objects.

All this exploring leads to learning – about the physical properties of things, about how objects work and can be related to other objects – really, about how the world works. Remember that young children learn by *doing*, and the younger the child, the more this is true. While your child explores, he learns about himself, too – what he can do and can't do, what he likes and dislikes. He also practises an enormous range of physical skills (also called motor skills). Hence the name: *sensorimotor*.

Most of the games in this book develop sensorimotor skills – and, quite deliberately, mental ones in the bargain.

—— DEVELOPMENTAL SUMMARY ——

The tiny newborn lies with clenched hands and tensed arms held close to the body; the 2-year-old confidently builds towers and solves puzzles. What has happened in the interval?

How a child handles toys, and what types of toys he enjoys at a particular age, follow fairly predictable patterns. Here's a quick summary of typical behaviour. I do mean quick, and I do mean *typical*. Remember that your baby – every baby – has his own rate and pattern of development. The age guidelines here reflect averages, and no individual baby is exactly average.

The Early Months

A newborn has little control over his hands, or over arm movements, so he explores primarily by *looking* (see Chapter 2, Early Eye-catchers).

He does automatically grasp something placed in his hand, though. This is a reflex that gives way to voluntary grasping over the next months. For fun, you might give your newborn light things to hold. At the moment he usually won't look at what he's holding, unless you draw his attention to it. Over the next few months he'll begin to co-ordinate eyes and hands to explore objects.

2 to 3 Months

Now your baby begins moving his arms with a bit of purpose. He enjoys batting a toy you dangle over him. Choose things that move and make sounds when he swats them. This batting and swatting are a preamble to the next stage of reaching with accuracy.

During this period a baby also begins to grasp toys voluntarily rather than merely as a reflex. He's a bit clumsy when making this transition— in fact, it may look like a step backwards as he drops things he used to hold so tightly. At first he usually grasps with his entire hand, his four fingers moving as one (as if he's wearing invisible

Babies a few weeks old automatically grasp any toy placed in their hands.

mittens). Later he'll use the fingers separately. Also, even though your baby holds things at will, he can't do much with them at this age.

4 Months

This is when a baby begins reaching for and grabbing toys with accuracy, expecially when he lies on his back and you dangle something over his chest. Initially he's clumsy – he misjudges the distance between hand and object, or maybe he just can't get his hand to go exactly where he wants it to go. But practice makes perfect. He also uses both hands together. (Later he'll reach and grasp with one hand only.) The best toys are easy to grab and hold – remember that his hands are pretty tiny.

Exploring toys with his mouth is also popular, but most 4-month-olds lack the eye–hand co-ordination needed to bring a toy to mouth without help. Early handling, too, still consists largely of holding and dropping.

5 Months

Now mouthing is probably his favourite pastime. At this age the baby easily brings things to the mouth, and keeps them there to extract every bit of information with his lips and tongue and cheeks. His

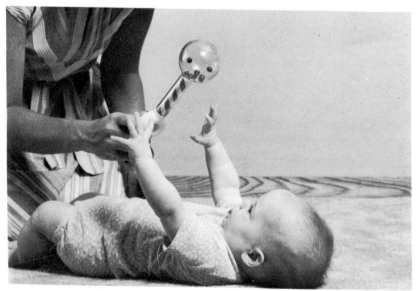

The 4-month-old reaches for toys you hold nearby.

mouth is an organ of touch, and at this age he can use it better than his hands to explore objects. Through mouthing he learns about size, shape and texture as well as taste.

Handling skills are better at this age, too. A baby drops things less often. He also begins holding things with his fingers rather than his entire hand. But on the whole he relies more on his mouth than his fingers to explore a toy. The best playthings are light, easy to grasp, and easy to clean.

6 to 9 Months

This is the real Age of Exploration, as mouthing (although still popular) takes a back seat to handling. A baby reaches for and grasps a toy with no problem, and once he has it in hand, he tries everything with it: shaking, waving, pulling, stretching, poking, folding, twisting. . . . He uses his entire hand, or just a few fingers if he wishes. It's amazing all the things he'll try with almost any object he gets his hands on.

A baby this age explores one object at a time, so one-piece toys are best. (However, if the toy has moving parts attached to one another, even better!) Successful toys move, change shape, and make intriguing sounds when he explores them. In fact, the more ways a toy responds to his handling, the more he enjoys it.

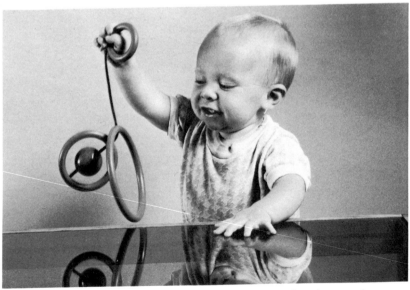

The 6- to 9-month-old loves toys that move and make sounds.

Near the end of this period he also likes exploring small parts inside larger ones, so hand-held transparent toys are popular, too.

10 to 12 Months

Crawling is such a thrill (new freedom!) that most beginning crawlers practically ignore handling objects for a time. Don't be surprised if you see a temporary lull in his interest in toys.

The 10- to 12-month-old still likes shaking, pulling and probing the one-piece toys so popular during the past few months, but he also starts enjoying toys that have several separate parts. He tries some preliminary ways of relating two parts, such as knocking them together, or holding them side by side to inspect their similarities and differences.

Grasping skills are so well developed that by this age most babies can pick up a small object between the thumb and forefinger (this is called the *pincer* grasp). Take heed, though – small objects are dangerous because they'll go straight into the mouth!

Toddlers between 12 and 18 months old like toys with parts that can be stacked, nested, fitted together in several different ways.

12 to 18 Months

The age of multi-part toys. The young toddler tries all kinds of experiments: filling a container with smaller objects and tipping them out again; fitting hoops over a pole; nesting a set of beakers inside one another; stacking up bricks; fitting two objects together and pulling them apart; solving simple puzzles.

What follows this? A slackening interest in exploring objects and the ways they relate for their own sake; a burgeoning interest in using objects to build things, or in fantasy play. Young children enjoy other toys and activities, too, like riding and sliding, looking at books and hugging a cuddly toy. All these are covered in different chapters.

———— BATTING AND SWATTING ————

Dangle a toy tantalizingly near your 2-month-old's hands. He spots it. Eyes widen. He gets excited, starts moving around, waves his fists haphazardly and – *wham!* He hits the toy. It moves. It makes sounds! He gets excited all over again, waves his fists –*wham!* Again and again. What baby power!

Does a 2-month-old deliberately hit the dangling toy? Does he realize that *he's* making the toy move and make sounds? That's debatable. Some psychologists believe it's a matter of circumstance: that is, the hanging toy excites the baby; in his excitement he moves about and accidentally hits it; the toy's sound and motion excite the baby all over again so that he moves and hits it . . . and the cycle goes on. All the baby knows is that he moves around and the toy moves around, like magic, with no direct connection between the two events.

Other researchers give the baby more credit. They believe that he has some elementary understanding of the relationship between his actions and the toy's, and that his hitting is more deliberate.

But it doesn't really matter. Most 2- to 3-month-olds *like* swatting at a dangling toy. It also provides early eye–hand co-ordination practice, and an important step towards reaching and grasping with accuracy, which will develop over the next few months.

This homemade Bat-a-Bag is great for batting games on the floor, on your lap or in a baby seat. Hold one end of the strap in each hand and dangle the bag portion near your baby's fists. The straps enable you to tie it across the pram or pushchair, too.

BAT-A-BAG

Ideal Intro Age: 2 months
Age Range: 2 to 4 months
FOR SUPERVISED PLAY ONLY

Tools and Materials

☆ Piece of colourful, patterned cloth, about 25 × 25 cm (10 × 10 in)

☆ Piece of elastic, about 2.5 cm (1 in) wide and 60 cm (24 in) long

☆ Small plastic container with lid (like an empty aspirin or pill bottle) with a few dried beans, screws or other rattling soundmakers inside

☆ Crumpled paper, for stuffing

☆ Sewing machine or needle and thread

Instructions

1. Fold the fabric in half, with the patterned sides (if any) facing each other. Stitch along the two short sides, making a long pouch.
2. Turn this pouch patterned-side-out and stuff with the aspirin bottle and crumpled paper.
3. Position the elastic along the open edge of the pouch as shown in the drawing. Stitch them together, simultaneously closing the bag and attaching the strap.

HINT: If you intend to hang this toy across your baby's pram, measure the pram before starting, to determine the length of elastic you need. The elastic must span the pram with enough left over to tie on to either side.

SAFETY NOTE: This toy is for batting only. The elastic makes it dangerous for a baby to play with if it's not attached to something or held by a parent.

Some Guidelines for Batting

1. Lay your baby on his back – on your lap, the sofa, the changing-table. Dangle a toy very near his fist and encourage him to bat it. Is he having trouble getting started? Tap the toy against his fist a few times.
2. When he's a bit more skilful, he'll bat at toys a little further away. He might also like batting toys when he's sitting on your lap or in a baby seat and you dangle an object in front of him.
3. Good batting toys include anything that:

    o is colourful – to attract your baby's attention in the first place;

    o is fairly light;

    o is large enough for your baby to hit easily; and

    o makes sounds when hit.

    Dangle the toy from your fingers or a short piece of ribbon. Remember: it should swing fairly freely.
4. For batting on the move, tie a toy across the pram or pushchair with a piece of elastic about 2.5 cm (1 in) wide.

Play Centres

A cot or cradle play centre is the traditional batting–reaching toy for the 2- to 5-month-old. Essentially, this is some kind of support (a rod, an arch) that spans the cot, and some toys (things to bat, grasp, pull on) that hang from it. There are a few good play centres in the shops at the moment. The best share these features:

o Easy adjustability! At first you'll want to hang the toys very low, close to your 2- to 3-month-old's hands for batting; then a little further away when he starts reaching with a purpose.

o The hanging toys should swing and make sounds when hit.

o At least some of the hanging toys should have a ring or handle that your baby can grasp easily.

SAFETY NOTE: *Never* tie any object across your baby's pram, cot or playpen once he can sit up or push up on hands and knees (usually at around 5 or 6 months). He might get tangled in it – with disastrous and heartbreaking results.

What about toys to bat and reach for out of the cot? After all, your baby usually prefers being near you when he's awake. When you're too busy to play batting and reaching games, perch him (in his baby seat or bouncer) in this homemade Play Box. It's a good place to practise reaching, grasping and other aspects of eye–hand co-ordination.

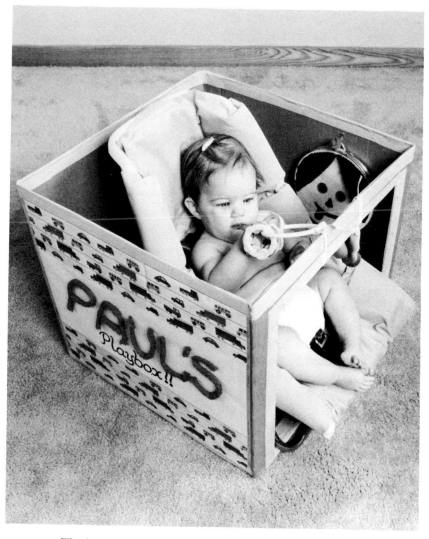

The homemade Play Box is a portable play centre that puts toys near your baby.

PLAY BOX

Ideal Intro Age: 3 months
Age Range: 3 to 6 months
FOR SUPERVISED PLAY ONLY

Tools and Materials

☆ Large cardboard box

☆ Short pieces of elastic or ribbon

☆ Small hand toys: rattles, things on rings, squeaky toys, etc.

☆ Packing or wrapping tape, about 3.8 cm (1½ in) wide (optional)

☆ Sharp knife or scissors

8 cm (3 ins)   CUT LINE

Instructions

1. Cut all the flaps off the top of the box.
2. Cut a large opening in one side, as shown. Make sure you leave about an 8 cm (3 in) cardboard frame around the three sides, to give the box strength.
3. If these cut surfaces are rough, line them with packing tape.
4. From the top 'arch' over the opening, hang a few hand toys on short pieces of elastic or ribbon. The length should be about 15 cm (6 in) maximum; your baby might get tangled in longer pieces.
5. Sit your baby in his baby seat, then place him, seat and all, in the box. Slide him forward far enough through the opening so that he can easily reach the dangling toys. What's nice about this set-up is that the weight of your baby and his seat holds the box steady as he plays.

HINTS

○ Hang things on the inner sides of the box for your baby to look at: a picture cut from a magazine (run tape around all four sides of the picture so your baby can't rip it off); or a homemade Eye Target (page 18); or cut a window in one side.

○ Invite older brothers or sisters to decorate this box with crayons or markers, or wrapping paper they can glue on.

○ You should probably discontinue using the Play Box when your baby can pull the hanging toys hard enough to threaten the walls with collapse.

SAFETY NOTE: Keep an eye on your baby any time he's in his baby seat, whether or not he's using his Play Box. He might get so active that he topples over and needs you to free him again. Also, as a general rule, *never* leave your baby in any kind of baby seat or bouncing cradle on a table, kitchen worktop or other raised surface. He just might wriggle off.

—REACHING AND GRABBING GAMES—

Starting around 4 months or so, your baby no longer just bats randomly at dangling toys. He reaches deliberately with open hands. And once he grabs something, he pulls on it or waves it about to make sounds. Try some reach-and-grab games. These are played just like the earlier batting games, except that the toys should have handles, rings or other protrusions your baby can grasp easily.

Let your baby reach for a dangling toy when lying on his back. When he grabs it, pull back slightly for some tug-of-war.

Sit your baby on your lap and dangle a toy in front of him. Or dangle it to one side, or up a little above his head, so he really has to stretch. But don't make it too hard to grab the toy – you want to challenge, not frustrate, your baby – and hold him securely so he doesn't tumble off your lap in his eagerness.

The homemade Grabbable Glove has plenty of convenient 'handles', and the strap lets you dangle it over your baby, or even tie it on to the cotside, cot play centre or pushchair.

GRABBABLE GLOVE

A super simple toy for reaching, grasping, exploring.
Ideal Intro Age: 4 months
Age Range: 3 to 9 months

Tools and Materials

☆ Colourful, small fabric glove (machine washable)

☆ Stuffing: polyester fibrefill, old tights, etc. (machine washable)

☆ Piece of elastic, about 2.5 cm (1 in) wide and 15 cm (6 in) long

☆ Sewing machine or needle and thread

Instructions

1. Stuff the glove tightly; make sure you force stuffing into the fingers and thumb.
2. Sew it closed.
3. Stitch on the elastic, as shown.

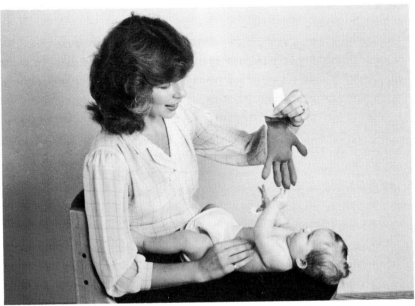

Use the homemade Grabbable Glove for reaching and grasping games.

Your baby will grab almost any object within reach, so make sure he doesn't have access to cups of hot liquids, small or sharp objects, or anything else that could be dangerous. He'll grab *you*, too: hair, face, glasses and jewellery. Many mothers I know find it convenient to switch from pierced earrings to clip-ons for the next few months. When he gives a really nasty tug on your hair, gently pry open his little hand with a mild reproach: 'No— that hurts. Be gentle.' He'll get the message eventually.

——— ACTIVE HANDS (AND MOUTH)! ———

Six months old already. For the next few months, your baby especially delights in playing with all kinds of toys.

A number of dramatic behavioural advances make this such a rich play era. One, your baby has developed good eye–hand co-ordination; he now reaches for objects quickly and confidently. Two, his grasping skills are vastly improved, so he uses fingers (as well as mouth) to explore the fine details of playthings. Three, his arm skills, too, are advanced. Now he can deliberately wave and shake objects to see what happens, or stretch an elastic toy between both hands, or pound a rattle against the floor to make as much noise as he can. All these arm and hand skills enable him to learn more about the properties of objects. And four, now he can probably sit all by himself, or very soon will. Among other things, this frees his hands and arms for play. Since he can't yet crawl, however, he's content to stay in one place, playing with anything within reach. When you combine all the above skills, they spell new play opportunities.

Most of the one-piece baby toys you find in shops are really designed for this age; there is a vast selection. The best toys inspire and respond to several skills: shaking, waving, poking, and so forth. Remember that sounds and movement are the most powerful rewards for babies of this age. As you shop, bear these guidelines in mind:

o Toys for this age should be one-piece, since a baby explores just one thing at a time. In fact, even if you give him a set of rattles that fit together, the chances are that he explores one, then the other, but doesn't try to relate them. Look for toys that have a few parts attached to one another, or that are hinged, so that as your baby plays, the toy flops around and changes shape.

○ A toy should be easy for your baby to get hold of, especially when he accidentally drops it — which he will, constantly. Toys that lie perfectly flat on the floor will be hard for him to pick up. Look for those in which some portion serves as a handle that is raised off the floor.

○ Plastic is an excellent material for this age. Most plastics are strong, light and easy to wash (remember that your baby will put into his mouth everything he gets his hands on). Wood is less successful, since it can splinter and tends to be heavy. Fabric toys are also good, provided that they are easy to grasp, flop about, and make sounds when your baby plays — and provided that they are machine washable. The homemade Triple Mittens and Talking Sock fit these criteria.

SAFETY NOTE: Toys should be free of sharp edges, holes small enough to trap a finger, or pinch points. If the toy has a squeaker, make sure it is so firmly attached that *you* can't pick it out. (If your baby does, he might choke on it.) Stuffed toys should have well-sewn seams, so that your baby can't get to the stuffing (and sometimes soundmakers) inside. Small features like eyes and decorations should, again, be so firmly attached that you can't pick them off. For this age group, embroidered or printed faces on soft toys are the safest. Toy safety laws should mean that anything made by a reputable company will be all right, but double-check yourself first to make quite sure.

Homemade Triple Mittens
are easy to grasp, pick up,
chew on.

TRIPLE MITTENS

This soft toy has plenty of parts for grasping and chewing on; and the protruding thumbs make it simple to pick up again when dropped.

Ideal Intro Age: 6 months
Age Range: 4 to 12 months

Tools and Materials

☆ 3 small child's mittens (machine washable)

☆ Stuffing material: polyester fibrefill, old tights, etc. (machine washable); or material that crackles when you squeeze and handle it:

cellophane sweet wrappers, some types of plastic carrier bags, or 1 or 2 Mylar balloons* (deflated)

☆ Sewing machine or needle and thread

Instructions

1. Stuff each mitten well with the stuffing material, leaving about 1.25 cm ($\frac{1}{2}$ in) unstuffed at the wrist.

2. Sew the mittens closed where the stuffing ends.

3. Sandwich the mittens together as shown, alternating the direction in which the thumbs point, and sew all three together at the wrists.

HINTS

○ Wash well in cold water and allow to dry naturally. The Mylar or cellophane might melt at high temperatures.

○ Save the remaining mitten to make a Beanbag (page 61).

Play Tips

Use these Triple Mittens in reach-and-grab games, too. When your baby is older, this is also a great soft 'ball' for throwing.

*Mylar (metallized polyester film) is a thick, shiny, cellophane-like material that's sometimes used to make helium-filled balloons. It is very strong and withstands machine washing. And it crackles tantalizingly when squeezed.

TALKING SOCK

Divide a sock into three or four sections — each one stuffed with a different type of soundmaker. The resulting squeezable, shakable soft toy flops about as your baby plays.

Ideal Intro Age: 6 months
Age Range: 6 to 12 months

Tools and Materials

☆ Woman's long cotton sock (with a lively design)

☆ Material that crackles when you squeeze and handle it; for example, some types of plastic carrier bags, cellophane sweet wrappers, a Mylar balloon (deflated). (See note on page 43)

☆ Small squeaky toy

☆ Small rattle, such as a ball or ring with beads or other soundmakers inside

☆ Strong thread (like embroidery thread)

Instructions

1. Stuff the toe of the sock with the crackly material. To keep it in place, wind a piece of embroidery thread around the sock a few times, then pull *tight* and tie with a double knot. Snip off the ends of the thread at the knot.

2. Next, stuff the rattle in the open sock, above the crackly material, and trap it in place with the thread, as above.

3. Similarly, stuff the squeaky toy in the sock and tie in place.

4. If there is any empty sock left, stuff the remaining portion with more crackly material (or even old tights), and close the top with a few loops of embroidery thread.

HINT: When it's time to wash this toy, snip through the thread loops, remove the contents, wash the sock, and stuff again.

SAFETY NOTE: Be sure you put the rattle (which is hard) in the middle of the sock, as described. If it's in one end, your child might hit himself with it as he waves the toy around by the other end.

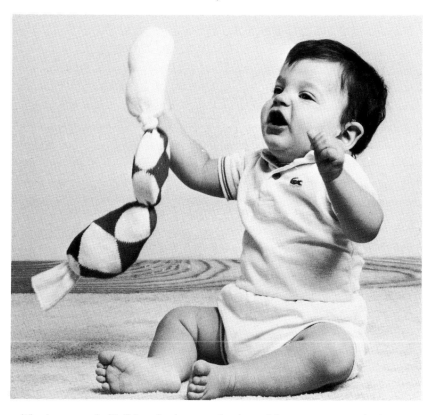

The homemade Talking Sock rewards play with movement and plenty of sounds.

Activity Centres

By definition, an activity centre mounts on the side of the cot and offers your child doors to open, knobs to twist, objects to slide, and so on. The best ones are pretty good toys – for the right age. Although most are marked for introduction at 6 months (or even younger), I've found that few children really play with an activity centre before 9 or 10 months. However, they continue to enjoy this type of toy well into toddlerhood.

Paper Play

Plain old paper is a favourite toy for the Explorer – it's easy to grasp, easy to crumple, fun to throw and tear. One baby I know delighted himself for an hour with an outdated telephone directory. Remember, though, always to supervise paper play; your baby might try to swallow – and consequently choke on – a ripped piece.

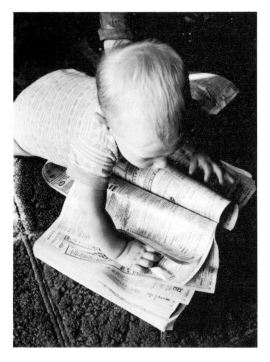

A discarded phone directory can keep your baby happily occupied (but be sure to supervise).

Explorer's Pool

The paddling pool is good for dry play indoors, too. Instead of water, fill it with several tantalizing toys, then your baby. The pool keeps everything clean and close at hand (remember: your baby will drop things a lot).

Play Tips

○ Baby throws a toy out of the pool . . . you retrieve it . . . he throws it again . . . you retrieve it . . . he throws again . . . you encourage him to throw *all* the toys out. Then you fill the pool for another round.

○ If you're willing to have a messy baby, empty out the toys and fill the pool with crumpled newspaper for your baby to thrash around in. He'll get dirty from the print, so be prepared with a bath. Stay close by to make sure he doesn't eat the paper.

○ Fill the pool with boulders of crumpled gift-wrapping paper. Be sure the type of paper is 'limp' enough so that it doesn't form sharp corners when compressed.

SAFETY NOTE: It's best always to supervise when your baby is playing in his Explorer's Pool, to make sure he doesn't climb or tumble out head first and hurt himself.

Play on the Move

For play on the move, attach a favourite toy to your baby's pushchair or carseat. Use a short piece of elastic or soft ribbon. Maximum length is about 15 cm (6 in); your baby could get tangled in a longer piece.

SAFETY NOTE: Never tie a toy – even a dummy – on a loop of string and put it around your baby's neck, like a necklace. He could get the cord caught on something, and strangle.

PEEKABOO

Starting at around 6 months, most babies adore games of peekaboo (or peep-bo, as some people call it). The versions are endless, but the principle is the same: a person 'disappears', then reappears accompanied by the jolly 'Peekaboo, I see you!' cry.

○ Baby's in his cot, you're nearby. Duck out of sight, then pop back into view: 'Peekaboo, I see you.'

○ Baby's lying on your lap, facing you. Cover your eyes with your hands: 'Where did Paul [*baby's name*] go? I can't see Paul.' Away come your hands and, 'There he is! Peekaboo, I see you.' For a twist, help your baby cover your eyes with *his* hands.

○ When he's fairly familiar with this game, your baby might like you to cover his eyes with your hand. Or help him cover his eyes with his own hands. Near the end of this first year, he might even cover and uncover his eyes all by himself. Or he'll hold his hands over his eyes and wait for you to pull them away with the 'peekaboo' exclamation.

○ Hide your face behind a toy, such as an Eye Target (page 18) or the Picture Parade (page 21). Then peep round it.

○ Cover your head with a nappy or towel, pause a second, then pull it off. Peekaboo! After a few rounds of this, your baby might like to snatch away the cover himself.

○ When your baby is 9 or so months old, try hiding *his* head under a nappy. (Being covered up usually frightens younger babies.) Make sure he's in a playful mood; initially he might not enjoy the surprise of being covered even at this age. Smile and giggle at the unveiling to let him know this is indeed a game. Once he catches on, he'll probably take the upper hand, covering his face all by himself and waiting for you to grab the nappy away (or doing it himself).

○ For giant-sized family games, one parent and baby hide under a blanket, and the other parent is the unveiler.

Toddler Games

Peekaboo games are still popular during the toddler years; and now that your child can walk, they can take on larger dimensions. For example, try some games of hide-and-seek – you hide somewhere in a room (behind a sofa or curtain) and call out for your toddler to find you.

Let your novice seeker watch you hide the first few times. He may need this clue to your whereabouts to be a successful sleuth. Also, he might not understand the purpose of the game straight away – that is, to find you again. So make it easy. In fact, you'll probably need to hide in the same room that he's in.

When both parents can play (or maybe a parent and an older child), try some real hide-and-seek games. One parent hides somewhere in the house or garden, and the other parent and toddler join forces to seek the missing player. Through this partnership your toddler picks up the game's fundamentals and will later search for the hidden player without a parent's side-by-side guidance. Reverse roles. This time, toddler and one parent hide somewhere, the other parent seeks. Giggles and conspiratorial whispers ('This is the best spot – Mum'll never look here') add to the fun.

For a special place to hide, and for all kinds of peeking play, make a special Peeking House.

PEEKING HOUSE

A scaled-up twist on a favourite game.
Ideal Intro Age: 15 months
Age Range: 15 to 36 months
(see page 50)

Tools and Materials

☆ Large cardboard carton   ☆ Scissors or sharp knife

☆ Packing tape (optional)

Instructions

1. Cut off one of the long sides of the box.
2. On the remaining sides, cut several peep holes – different sizes and shapes if you like. Just make sure that every hole is too small for your child to fit his head through.
3. Cover any rough edges with tape, to prevent scratches.

HINT: Your older child – or even your toddler, if he's into crayons and markers – can decorate the box.

Play Tip

Stand the box up, with the open side to the back. Your toddler sneaks behind and peekaboos out. You peekaboo back. Alternatively, he might want to hide *under* the box and peek out.

Decorate your
homemade Peeking
House any way you
wish.

Peekaboo and Separation Anxiety

One reason peekaboo is so popular is that it links nicely to a facet of emotional development.

Starting at some time after 6 months, many babies become quite distressed when separated from their parents. It doesn't matter whether you're going out for the evening or just to the garage – as soon as you make a move for the door your baby is clingy and grief-stricken.

This behaviour is commonly called *separation anxiety*. It might baffle you, especially if your baby used to let you come and go without much notice. There are times it probably annoys you, too, when you're in a hurry and your baby won't let you go.

It's natural that you might mutter to yourself, 'This is ridiculous – he knows I'm coming back soon.'

But in a way he doesn't.

By 6 or 7 months he *does* realize how much he loves and needs you – a positive step in your lifelong love affair. But here's the rub. Just as he's realizing his dependence on you, he also begins realizing that you can leave, that you're not always available. And when you're not there, he feels abandoned. It's a big realization for such a small, relatively helpless person!

Nor does he truly realize you will always return. At this age a baby doesn't fully understand *object permanence*: that things, including people, which disappear can reappear. (Understanding of this concept develops during the latter half of this year. You can help your baby

Peekaboo games may help your child work through separation anxiety.

learn with peekaboo and the Hiding and Finding Toys games in the next section.) In his mind, an object ceases to exist once it leaves his sight. So each time you leave, he can't really rely on your reappearance. No wonder he feels anxious.

With time and experience of your comings and goings (and of things disappearing and reappearing), your baby learns that you can, indeed, be depended on to come back. His separation anxiety will diminish, then disappear. He might go through similar spells during toddlerhood, too. As his love for you grows greater still, there are times your absence will make him insecure.

Peekaboo is really a way of acting out separations and reunions, but in a pleasant, non-threatening context. It's also a situation your baby helps control (unlike your real leavings). It's fun to control things yourself when so much of your life is controlled by others. Some psychologists believe that peekaboo games can even help a baby work through some of his anxiety.

HIDING AND FINDING TOYS

You hide a toy, your baby finds it. 'Good for you, clever Jason!' you say. He's so proud of himself.

Like peekaboo, this basic game has endless varieties and, like peekaboo, it can help your child understand object permanence. And, again like peekaboo, it's fun.

Most babies start to enjoy hiding-and-finding games at around 8 or 9 months, the typical age when they're beginning to grasp object permanence. A younger baby typically loses interest in a toy that leaves his sight. Make sure your baby watches you hide the toy, otherwise he won't understand that he's supposed to find it again. If your baby is new to this game, you might leave part of the hidden toy exposed, as a not-so-subtle clue.

Good Hiding Places

o Under something – nappy, towel, inverted plastic bowl or small box, your hands, etc.

○ Inside something – a box with a flip-up top (like a cigar box) or a loosely fitting top (like a shoebox), a large boot, a cooking pot with matching lid, etc.

○ Behind something – your back (baby crawls around you to retrieve the hidden toy).

Toddler Games

1. Loosely wrap a toy in a piece of paper (especially ordinary wrapping paper). Let your child open his 'present'. Add to the festivities with a chorus of 'Happy Birthday'.
2. Take two differently coloured hand towels. Hide a toy under one of them. Can your toddler find it easily? Try three towels.
3. Take two containers (such as the largest cups from a set of stacking/nesting beakers). Hide a small toy under one of them. Can your toddler find it easily? Shuffle the cups around.

—— EXPLORING TEXTURES ——

Texture, just like sound and colour, is a physical property of an object, and one that most babies enjoy exploring. Your baby will probably stroke and finger his toys (especially cloth ones), the carpet, your clothing, almost anything he gets his hands on. Add variety with these texture toys and games:

1. Take your baby on a 'texture tour' of your home. Let him feel things such as curtains, water rushing from a tap, bumpy bedspreads, fluffy towels. Try to describe the textures as best you can (some will really tax your vocabulary and imagination).
2. Try a 'texture walk' outdoors, too, pausing frequently so your child can feel the rough bark of trees, smooth leaves, prickly grass shoots, brick walls, signposts. . . .

The following homemade texture toys provide him with a variety of textures to explore at a sitting.

The homemade Touchable Glove gives your baby five textures to explore at once.

TOUCHABLE GLOVE

You wear this glove, and your baby explores each textured finger.
Ideal Intro Age: 6 months
Age Range: 6 to 12 months

Tools and Materials

☆ Large glove

☆ Fabric scraps – choose a variety of textures

☆ Needle and thread

Instructions

Sew a scrap of fabric firmly on to each of the glove's fingers.

Play Tips

Use this glove to give your baby a textural massage.

TEXTURE CARDS

Ideal Intro Age: 9 months (a younger baby would probably rather suck or chew these cards than feel them)
Age Range: 9 to 36 months
(see page 56)

Tools and Materials

☆ Several report cards, each about 20 × 12.5 cm (8 × 5 in); or other pieces of cardboard

☆ The same number of different-textured fabric scraps: corduroy, towelling, flannel, felt, velvet, etc.

☆ Short piece of ribbon

☆ All-purpose household glue (non-toxic)

☆ Scissors and, if available, hole punch

Instructions

1. Glue a different fabric on each card, covering it completely. Trim off any excess.
2. Punch or poke a hole in the upper right-hand corner of each card; tie the cards together loosely with a small loop of ribbon.

SAFETY NOTE: Supervise play if your baby is under a year old. He might try to tear off the fabric and put it (or the card) into his mouth.

Talk about the different
textures on these
homemade Texture Cards.

A homemade Texture Book
is great for your toddler.

TEXTURE BOOK

Ideal Intro Age: 12 months
Age Range: 12 to 36 months

Tools and Materials

☆ Blank scrapbook; buy one or make one from sheets of cardboard

☆ Textured materials: e.g.

○ Fabric scraps

○ Fine-grained sandpaper

○ Short pieces of ribbon

○ Squares of corrugated cardboard

○ Old greetings cards with glitter or embossed surfaces

○ Textured wallpaper samples (especially flocked)

☆ All-purpose household glue (non-toxic)

Instructions

Glue a few textured objects on each page of the book.

SAFETY NOTE: Avoid small things (like cotton wool balls) that might be a hazard if your toddler should rip them off a page.

SURPRISE TOUCH BOX

Here's a surprise way your older toddler can explore objects just by touch. Put a textured object inside the Surprise Touch Box and replace the lid. Your child reaches in through the hole and feels it. You might even ask him to guess what he's touching.

Ideal Intro Age: 24 months
Age Range: 24 to 36 months
(see page 58)

Tools and Materials

☆ Adult-sized shoebox with lid

☆ Clear adhesive tape, about 2.5 cm (1 in) wide

☆ Scissors

Instructions

1. Cut a tunnel-shaped opening in one end of the box. Make sure it is large enough to accommodate your child's hand easily.

2. Line the cut edges with tape to prevent scratches.

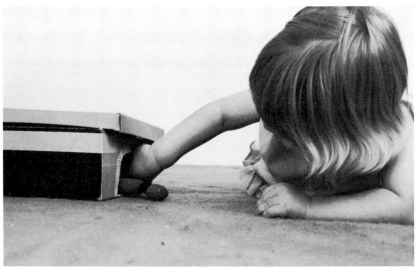

With this homemade Surprise Touch Box, your toddler explores
objects just by feel.

PUTTING IT TOGETHER

At some point between 9 and 12 months, your baby no longer plays
with one thing at a time. Maybe he hits two rattling toys together to
see what happens, or he puts a small object into a larger one. This is a
beginning. Over the next year or so he'll try all kinds of things, like
building towers (and knocking them over), filling a container and
emptying it again, fitting things together, solving simple puzzles . . .
all kinds of things. Now he prefers toys that have several different
pieces.

One reason he loves multi-part playthings is because the 1-year-old
is fascinated with organization and connection— what goes with what.

At this age your child is making more sense out of the world. He
realizes that there is a logical order to many things. For example, he's
beginning to understand what familiar objects are used for – a cup is
for drinking out of, shoes are for wearing on the feet. He also realizes
that certain objects belong in particular places – his socks go in the
drawer, books and toys on the nursery shelves. (Unfortunately for you,
he probably won't put his things away at this age, but he is beginning
to understand where they should go.)

Once your child begins talking, you'll notice this fascination even
more clearly. He loves to connect words with objects, and will con-

stantly be asking you, 'What's dat?' He also delights in connecting people with their possessions, and will croon on about Daddy's shoes and Mummy's shoes and 'My shoes!'

His interest in organization naturally extends to his play. That's why he spends countless hours exploring the ways in which he can organize the parts of a toy: stack them, fit them together, put one part inside or under another part. Through these experiments he also learns important concepts like size differences and spatial relationships (inside, under, on top of), especially when you supply the appropriate words as you and he play: 'Good for you – you put the brick inside the box.' And into the bargain, he practises precise eye–hand co-ordination.

However, he hasn't left behind totally the play of the baby months. He still shakes and mouths and otherwise explores objects. Many favourite baby toys of the past few months continue to delight him.

Here are some of the most popular multi-part toys and games (and some things you can make, too).

Fill and Empty

The most popular early activity is putting objects into some kind of container, taking or tipping them out, then repeating the process – sometimes for long stretches. This Fill and Empty play is fairly mistake-proof: the opening in the container is much larger than the objects that go inside. It's also a forerunner of fitting things together, like a shape sorter, that requires more precision.

GOOD CONTAINERS: Plastic mixing bowl, small cardboard box, large plastic food storage container, empty coffee tin (make sure the cut edge isn't sharp!).

GOOD FILLERS: Plastic pop beads, coasters (an absolute favourite), balls, bricks, rattles, and other favourite small baby toys.

GOOD GAMES:
1. Try Fill and Empty on a grand scale, with a big box or plastic laundry basket and an assortment of good-sized toys, especially stuffed animals. Have a race – you throw toys into the box, your toddler throws them out as quickly as he can.
2. A good game for tidy-up time: encourage your toddler to put large toys into an even larger container. Since he has to stand up to play, and

maybe even toddle around the room to gather ammunition, his whole body is involved in the game.

GOOD HOMEMADE TOYS: These homemade Fill and Empty toys — Sock Beanbags, Container Bank, Posting Cards — are designed for different skill levels.

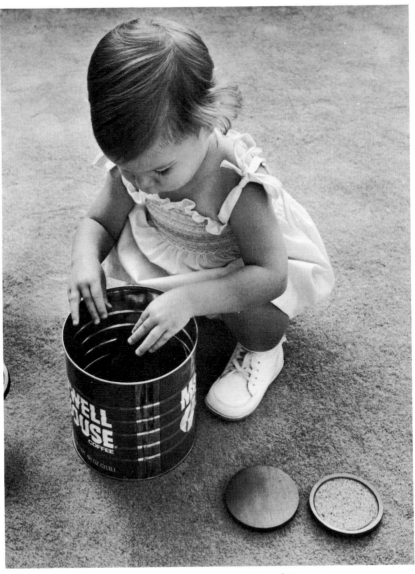

A coffee tin and coasters are super Fill and Empty toys.

SOCK BEANBAGS

Homemade Sock Beanbags are great for Fill and Empty. They're easy to pick up because they 'mould' to your toddler's hand.

Ideal Intro Age: 12 months

Age Range: 12 to 36 months

Tools and Materials

For each beanbag:

☆ Sturdy child's sock

☆ Dried beans

☆ Scissors

☆ Sewing machine or needle and thread

Instructions

1. Fill the foot section of a sock with beans.
2. Snip off the remaining portion of the sock about 2.5 cm (1 in) above the beans.
3. Turn the cut edges inside the sock (this will prevent unravelling) and sew the sock closed. Use a double or triple row of stitches to make sure the beans can't escape; if your toddler gets his hands on them he might swallow them or stuff them up his nose.

HINT: Instead of a sock, use a child's mitten.

Play Tips

○ Give your baby a few Sock Beanbags and a plastic mixing bowl or a small cardboard box.

○ These beanbags are also good stacking toys, because they sit on top of one another any way your toddler puts them.

○ He can also use them as toys to throw in the homemade Target Practice (page 109).

CONTAINER BANK

This is a favourite because toddlers love the challenge of fitting
things through a slot, and because the coasters make such a terrific
clanking sound when they hit the metal coffee tin (see Safety Note).
Supervise play the first few times to make sure your toddler knows
how to remove the lid once he has inserted the coasters.

Ideal Intro Age: 15 months
Age Range: 15 to 30 months

Tools and Materials

☆ Large, empty coffee tin   ☆ Sharp knife
  with plastic lid

☆ Set of coasters

Instructions

In the plastic lid, cut a slot long and wide enough for the coasters to
fit through easily. Line the slot with tape if the edges are sharp.

SAFETY NOTE: If the coffee tin has a sharp edge where the metal lid
was cut off, hammer it smooth. If you can't, discard the coffee tin
and use a plastic food storage container. It won't make as much
noise, but it'll be fun just the same. Also, the coasters should be at
least 5 cm (2 in) in diameter; this size, at least according to some
toy safety standards, is too large to fit entirely into your toddler's
mouth.

POSTING CARDS

This Fill and Empty game uses playing cards – popular with most older toddlers – which give you plenty of opportunities for reinforcing other skills.
Ideal Intro Age: 18 months
Age Range: 18 to 36 months
(see page 64)

Tools and Materials

☆ Deep adult-sized shoebox, with lid

☆ Masking or packing tape, about 3.8 cm (1½ in) wide

☆ Pack of ordinary playing cards

☆ Scissors or sharp knife

Instructions

1. Cut a slot in the lid of the shoebox. It should be at least 2.5 cm (1 in) longer than the cards, and at least 1.25 cm (½ in) wide.
2. Line the slot on all four sides with the tape to prevent tears.

Play Tips

From 18 months:

○ Show your toddler how to insert cards through the slot one by one, then how to open the box, tip out its contents, and start again. Make it fun; pretend you're sending postcards to friends ('Let's post this one to Granny Palmer'), or putting notes into a bank ('Here goes another note into our account – soon we'll have enough to buy those silver sandals').

NOTE: You might give your toddler just a partial pack; inserting all fifty-two cards may be overwhelming.

○ Alternate turns: he inserts a card, you insert a card, he inserts a card. . . . This helps him learn social rules like taking turns.

From 24 months:

(Use just the aces, twos and threes.)

○ Help your toddler count the spots on each card before he inserts it. Great for early counting skills.

○ Lay all twelve cards face up on the floor. Pick up one card (say, a three), and ask your toddler to find all the other cards that have the same number of spots, then to insert them into the box.

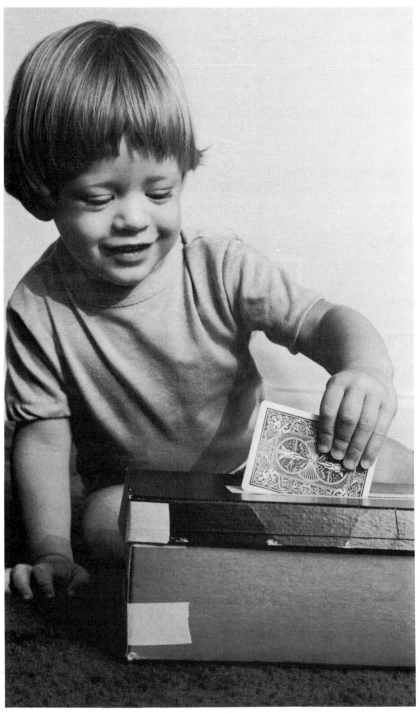

This homemade Posting Cards toy is ideal for Fill and Empty games.

Nesting toys help your toddler learn size differences and spatial relationships.

Nesting Toys

Nesting two containers (that is, putting the smaller into the larger) which are close in size requires more dexterity and discrimination than simple Fill and Empty. You can buy sets of inexpensive plastic nesting beakers; they're well worth it because they'll be used in all kinds of play, including water and sand. Choose beakers that also stack securely on one another when inverted.

HINT: The first few times your toddler plays with nesting beakers, he might prefer using just a few— say, the largest, the middle size, and the smallest. Add more as his skill increases.

SAFETY NOTE: The smallest beaker in the set should be too large to fit into your toddler's mouth. If it can fit, however, throw it away.

Stacking Toys

These include anything from stacking/nesting beakers to bricks that fit on top of one another, from beanbags to special stacking opportunities built into toys that have other purposes as well. Most toddlers love to stack toys into towers. And knock them down. And stack them up.

Individual Differences

In building towers, just like in playing with any of the toys in this chapter (and, really, throughout this book), each toddler has his own style. I've seen some children who are too impatient (at first) to create tall towers. They stack up just two or three items – or even urge a parent to – then knock the short tower over and start again; or they rush through building, no matter how high they go, just to get to the destruction phase. Other toddlers work slowly and methodically. These persistent builders often test how high they can go. Some get a little annoyed when the tower falls – or when you knock it over, even in play. So if your toddler doesn't seem interested in tower building, or rushes through it, or plods along, or gets angry when things don't go according to plan, don't worry; these are all natural responses.

A Research Study

At what age does stacking begin? How high a tower is typical at any given age? These, obviously, depend on the toys, because some are easier to stack than others.

It seems that stacking (again, like most play with toys) requires a meshing of physical and mental skills. On the physical side, your child has to be able to place the second toy on top of the first *and* let go without knocking the toy off. That final step's the hard part, and one reason why early stacking attempts can be rather clumsy. I've found that toddlers are more successful if the stacking objects fit together loosely – say, a tapered end into a hollow – rather than merely rest on each other.

On the mental side, the child has to be able to conceive of vertical space, and realize that his towers, indeed, can go as high as his physical skills will allow. For a toddler whose play with toys has largely been horizontal, that's no small step.

Because developmental psychologists feel that conceiving of space vertically is an important behavioural milestone, they've examined tower building in young children. One definitive study, conducted by Arnold Gesell more than forty years ago, found the following:

At 12 months:

o 16 per cent of the toddlers built a tower two bricks high; none built a higher one.

At 18 months:

o 100 per cent of the children built two-brick-high towers;

○ 92 per cent built three-brick towers;

○ 77 per cent built four-brick towers;

○ 44 per cent built five-brick towers;

○ 27 per cent built six-brick towers.

At 24 months:

○ 100 per cent built two- and three-brick towers;

○ 97 per cent built four-brick towers;

○ 85 per cent built five-brick towers;

○ 76 per cent built six-brick towers.

At 36 months:

○ 100 per cent of the children built towers two, three and four bricks high;

○ 97 per cent built towers five and six bricks high.

These are only guidelines, though. The bricks Dr Gesell used were identical 2.5-cm (1-in) cubes – which, incidentally, are so small they're dangerous for a toddler to play with unsupervised. You're bound to see differences in your own child's skill based partly on the toys he uses.

Stacking Hoops on a Pole

A set of plastic doughnut-like hoops that fit on a pole is another traditional toy that's well worth buying, although not necessarily for the reasons for which it was originally designed.

The hoops will get plenty of play by themselves – as teethers, for throwing, as small toys for Fill and Empty and Hiding and Finding Toys games. Yes, your toddler will probably place a few over the pole (especially if you demonstrate and encourage), but rarely in order. The size difference from one hoop to the next is just too fine for most toddlers to discriminate between. Don't expect perfection.

If your toddler likes trying, give him just three hoops – largest, middle-sized and smallest. Add more as skills improve.

HINT: A stacking hoops set is also one of the single best toys for teaching colours. Most plastic versions are quite inexpensive, too.

Early Fitting Toys

In the toy shop you'll find lots of toddler items in which one part, often a character, fits into another – a car, a boat, some kind of base. These usually work well. They're even better if the figures can somehow fit together end to end. In fact, fitting objects, like hollow pegs, together end to end is one of the most popular activities I've witnessed in play labs. Not many toys incorporate this feature, so look hard.

Bricks and Construction

Wooden bricks are usually more popular after 24 months than before. The younger toddler is just as happy with all the other types of fitting-stacking-nesting toys described before. Some toddlers don't use bricks much before 36 months.

Some toddlers like simple construction-type toys at 24 months, but it really depends on the particular toy. It's best to buy a small set of some modular system to start. Then, when your toddler proves his interest, expand the number of pieces.

Giant Homemade Blocks

Toddlers of all ages do like large, light blocks, though: for building, for crawling over, for using as chairs. One reason giant blocks are popular is because the not-so-large toddler feels powerful and impor-tant merely carrying them. What a great accomplishment it is, too, to build massive structures when you're not yet very massive yourself! The homemade Cardboard Blocks and Brown Paper Bag Blocks pro-vide plenty of play. Some suggested games:

From 15 months:

o Stack a few blocks into a tower for your toddler to knock over. *Kaboom!* Go faster . . . faster. Who's faster – the construction company or the demolition expert?

o Help your toddler to build his own towers, too – a great way to enhance eye–hand co-ordination.

From 18 months:

○ You build a tower or wall of blocks; he then bulldozes it flat on his favourite riding toy.

○ With enough blocks you can even build forts and fantasy hideouts.

○ Your older toddler (or his older brother or sister) might like to decorate these finished blocks with crayons or (non-toxic) felt-tipped markers.

SAFETY NOTE: Since these blocks are made with paper and tape, it's best to introduce them after your toddler is past the stage where he rips up and eats paper, or picks at and eats tape.

CARDBOARD BLOCKS

Wonderful cardboard blocks made from large cartons from supermarkets.

Ideal Intro Age: 18 months

Age Range: 15 to 36 months

Tools and Materials

For each block you need:

☆ Large cardboard carton with flaps on the top

☆ Plenty of newspaper

☆ Wrapping or packing tape, at least 3.8 cm ($1\frac{1}{2}$ in) wide

☆ Hammer (optional)

Instructions

1. Fill the box to overflowing with balls of crumpled newspaper (for added sturdiness), press the paper down, and tape the top flaps closed.

2. If the corners feel sharp, pound them smooth with the hammer.

BROWN PAPER BAG BLOCKS

These large, lightweight, surprisingly durable and *free* blocks won't damage walls, furniture or other children should your toddler throw them. Make plenty.

Ideal Intro Age: 18 months
Age Range: 15 to 36 months

Tools and Materials

For each block you need:

☆ Brown paper grocery bag

☆ Newspaper – about 14 double-page sheets

☆ Packing or wrapping tape, at least 3.8 cm ($1\frac{1}{2}$ in) wide

Instructions

1. Remove handles, if any, from bag. Lay the closed bag on a flat, hard surface, fold over the top about 20 cm (8 in) and crease *well*.
2. Open the bag, stand it up, and fill nearly to the top with crumpled newspaper balls.
3. Press down the crumpled paper, fold over the top of the bag on the crease line, and tape it closed.

HINT: Experiment with the number of newspaper balls you need to stuff a bag fairly firmly. It might be more or fewer than the recommended fourteen, depending on the size of bag you use.

Play Tip

Hold your toddler's hand and help him kick a block like a ball. It won't roll away – so kick it again . . . and again. When he's a good kicker, race each other kicking blocks around the room.

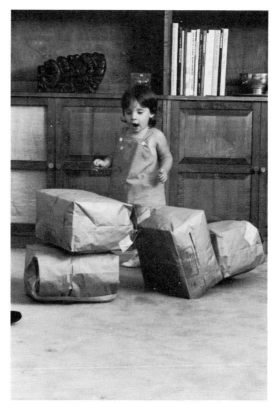

These homemade giant Brown Paper Bag Blocks are light, durable and packed with play possibilities.

Puzzles

Teachers and playgroup leaders swear by puzzles because, as they themselves have pointed out, puzzle play has so many benefits. For example, it builds eye–hand co-ordination; it helps develop concepts like size, shape and spatial orientation (which side is up?); and it helps a child understand how separate parts of an object make up the whole. The forced correctness of puzzles also offers nice contrast to the freer-range toys that have no one way to use them correctly.

Toddler tray puzzles come in two main types:

○ *Island puzzles*, in which each removable piece is a complete object that fits into its own well in the puzzle tray.

○ *Jigsaw puzzles*, in which each piece is a component of a whole, and all the pieces fit into the same large, shallow well.

A toddler is usually ready for three- or four-piece island puzzles by about 18 months. He probably needs help completing them, though.

Simple jigsaw puzzles are usually introduced to toddlers of between 24 and 36 months.

When buying puzzles, bear these things in mind:

○ Look for sturdiness. Favourite puzzles are worked and reworked endlessly and must be able to stand up to this.

○ Pieces must be easy to remove. Knobs and other handles help.

○ In a jigsaw puzzle, each piece should be recognizable when removed from the frame; that is, on a 'person' puzzle, the leg should look like a leg, not a misshapen blob.

Homemade People Puzzles

These can't match commercial ones in durability, but they make up for it in personality.

Initially this type of jigsaw puzzle may be hard for your child to complete, since it doesn't have a tray that helps him place the pieces; but the familiarity of the subject will give him clues.

Homemade People Puzzles can help your toddler learn component parts of an object – even himself.

When you and your toddler play together, talk about the people in the puzzles: who they are (if a family member), the parts of the face and body, what they're wearing, what they might be holding. If the puzzle people are wearing uniforms, talk about these and the jobs they go with, too. And if the puzzle is your toddler's picture — well, you have plenty to talk about.

PEOPLE PUZZLES

Ideal Intro Age: 24 months
Age Range: 24 to 36 months

Tools and Materials

☆ Picture of a person, about 25 × 20 cm (10 × 8 in); cut one from a magazine — or get a snap of your toddler enlarged and use that

☆ Sheet of thin cardboard, same size

☆ All-purpose household glue (non-toxic)

☆ Scissors

Instructions

1. Coat the back of the picture with glue. (Easy way: pour some glue into a saucer, dilute slightly with water, and paint on to the picture with a damp paper towel.) Attach to the cardboard.
2. When the glue dries, cut the picture into a few pieces.

HINT: Look for a large, simple picture, ideally showing the whole person. Cut it out along natural breaks; that is, maybe divide into head, torso and legs. These divisions give your toddler clues for reconstruction. Also, the cuts should be wavy lines so that the pieces slide together, not fit like traditional adult jigsaw pieces. Is the puzzle too easy? Cut into some more pieces. Is it too hard? Tape some pieces back together.

Biscuit-cutter Puzzle

Most toddlers love holidays — especially Christmas and Easter. If you have any plastic biscuit or pastry cutters in the shapes of holiday-related items, you can use them to make a homemade island puzzle that will have special meaning.

This toy is recommended for a child of 24 months old because the shapes will probably be a little harder for him to fit than traditional island puzzle pieces.

BISCUIT-CUTTER PUZZLE

Ideal Intro Age: 24 months
Age Range: 24 to 36 months

Tools and Materials

☆ Set of plastic biscuit or pastry cutters; make sure they don't have sharp edges

☆ 2 sheets of corrugated or other fairly thick cardboard, about 25 × 20 cm (10 × 8 in); you can cut these from a large cardboard box

☆ Sheet of coloured paper

☆ Pencil

☆ Stanley knife (also called a hobby knife)

☆ All-purpose household glue (non-toxic)

☆ Clear adhesive tape, at least 2.5 cm (1 in) wide

Instructions

1. Trace the biscuit-cutter shapes on one piece of cardboard.
2. Carefully cut them out, using the Stanley knife.
3. Sandwich the sheets of coloured paper between the two sheets of cardboard, and glue all three together.
4. Run tape around the entire perimeter.

HINT: You can use foam core board instead of the cardboard; it's easy to cut and looks terrific. Ask for it at art supply shops.

The familiar shapes of this homemade Biscuit-cutter Puzzle give it special meaning.

EARLY ART SUPPLIES

Many toddlers of 18 to 24 months and up enjoy crayons, play dough and other basic art materials. At this age they're more interested in the process than the product, and in dabbling for a few minutes, not working industriously to create a masterpiece. In other words, it's not the time to ask your child to draw a landscape for you. Also, since toddlers aren't the most careful of creatures, you should stay nearby to confine his creative urges to the page rather than the wall.

The following materials suit most toddlers.

Crayons

Choose jumbo crayons about 1.25 cm ($\frac{1}{2}$ in) in diameter. These are easier for a toddler to hold (he usually grasps them like a drumstick), and less likely to break. The non-rolling type stay close at hand. Make sure crayons are non-toxic — your toddler will probably put them into his mouth. When he does, remove the crayon while reminding him that crayons are for drawing with, not eating. He'll learn this rule after a few attempts.

Give your toddler large sheets of paper to draw on. Best is a giant pad, available at an art supply shop — it holds the page steady and gives him plenty of room. You can keep single sheets stationary by taping them to the drawing surface — highchair tray or table top.

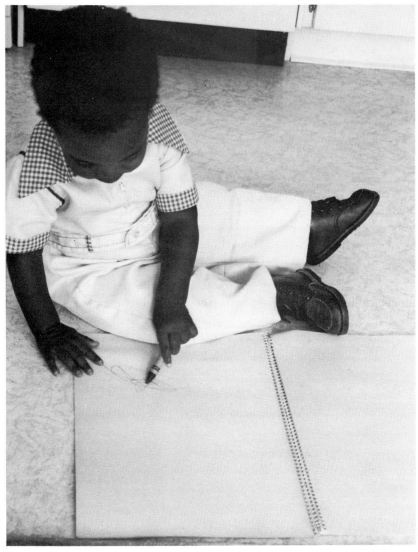

Give your toddler a big pad and jumbo crayons for his scribbling fun.

Play Tips

o   Draw side by side. Many parents I know say that their toddlers love watching them draw, even if the parent isn't much of an artist. Ask him what he would like you to draw.

o   Draw an object and ask your toddler to guess what it is.

o   Let your toddler colour (really, scribble) in the shapes you've drawn.

Felt-tipped Markers

These beat crayons hands down – they make much more dramatic, colourful scribbles – but they are messier. Choose only non-toxic ones, and make sure your toddler no longer chews his art supplies. Supply *large* sheets of paper. It's also a good idea to protect the floor or table top with newspaper or a plastic cloth. He might sometimes miss his drawing pad.

Chalk

A blackboard and coloured chalks make a nice, fairly clean set of art materials. Select the thickest chalks you can find, but expect breakages nonetheless.

Finger Paints

Finger paints are great for the toddler who loves to make a mess (as most toddlers do). Try giving yours this fake finger paint to see whether he likes the idea – and can be trusted to confine the sloppiness to a small setting:

○ Beat soap flakes (NOT powdered detergent) with water and some food colouring to make a smooth paste.

Your toddler can finger paint on a baking tray, the highchair tray, or directly on any table that sponges clean. Or let him paint in the bath – easy to clean!

If he enjoys this, he's probably ready for the real thing. You can buy jars of finger paint (non-toxic) at toy and art supply shops. He can paint on any glossy paper, such as coated shelf paper or special finger paint paper. Dampen the paper with a sponge, add a blob of paint (one colour is fine), and stay close by to make sure he doesn't redecorate the room. When he's finished, let the painting dry, then display it on the refrigerator (the ideal home art gallery).

Play Dough

At this age your toddler won't make specific objects. Rather, he'll love just squishing and squeezing and pounding the dough, or making shapes in it with objects like biscuit-cutters. Again, be sure to supervise so that dough doesn't end up in his hair – or worse.

PLAY DOUGH

Ideal Intro Age: 24 months
Age Range: 24 to 36 months

Tools and Materials

☆ 255 g (9 oz) plain flour

☆ 170 g (6 oz) salt

☆ 142 ml (4 fl oz) water

☆ 22 ml (1½ tblsp) cooking or salad oil

☆ Food colouring

☆ Mixing bowl

Instructions

1. Mix together the flour and salt.
2. Add the water and oil, and knead well until the mixture is smooth (about 10 minutes or so).
3. Add the food colouring and knead until the colour is fully blended.
4. Store in a plastic bag in the refrigerator.

HINT: You might need to add a bit more flour or water until the consistency is smooth but not sticky. Each time I make this dough, I have to vary the proportions slightly.

Poster Paints

These, too, can be fun but messy. Many parents I know confine painting to school. If you want to try at home, make sure your child wears a smock (one of your shirts, worn backwards, does the trick), and that the floor around the easel is protected with lots of newspaper or a plastic cloth. Alternatively, let your toddler paint outside. Drips and spills there will be less destructive. A toddler copes best with brushes that have bristles about 2.5 cm (1 in) or more across. He might also like to use a piece of sponge instead of a brush, but make sure he doesn't chew it.

For a cleaner version of outdoor painting, give your toddler a decorator's paintbrush and a bucket of water, and let him paint your house or front path. It disappears – magic!

A brush and a bowl of water make a novel (and non-destructive) outdoor 'paint' set.

BALLPOINT PAINT PEN

This homemade art material is a fairly clean way to paint. In essence, it's a giant ballpoint pen. Your child can roll it across *large* sheets of paper to make dazzling scribbles.

Ideal Intro Age: 24 months
Age Range: 24 to 36 months
(see page 80)

Tools and Materials

☆ Empty roll-on deodorant bottle, with a removable top

☆ Finger paint or poster paint

Instructions

1. Prise the top off the bottle and wash the bottle thoroughly.
2. Fill with paint that's diluted with water, and replace the top.

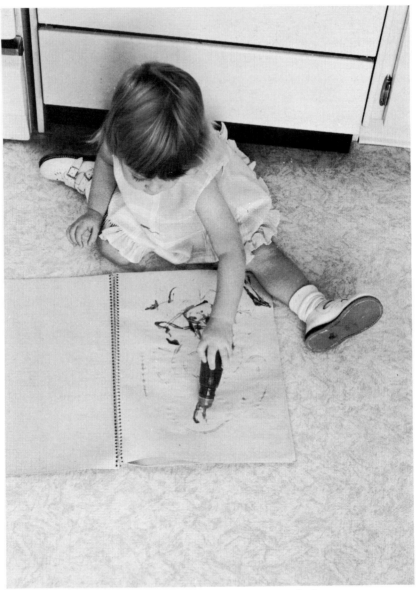

The homemade Ballpoint Paint Pen is made from an
empty deodorant bottle.

─── TO SUM UP ───

That's it for hands and heads. Of course, you and your child will
undoubtedly devise your own toys and games— good for you! Now let's
look at activities for the entire body. On to exercise.

active play and exercise 4

Active play means kicking, sitting, crawling, walking and running, jumping, climbing and sliding, throwing a ball, riding a ride-on, hitting a punching bag. Psychologists generally call these the large-muscle or *gross-motor skills*, in contrast to the *fine-motor skills* covered in Chapter 3, Activities for Hands (and Heads).

The younger the child, the more she welcomes your participation in these skills. The newborn has relatively little control over her large muscles and looks to you for nearly all physical activity. As a baby develops skills—for example, sitting, crawling, walking—she partici-pates increasingly in gross-motor play. In fact, unlike many adults, she rarely needs encouragement; the sheer joy of movement is induce-ment enough.

Even so, you play an important role in your child's large-muscle activities. She needs you to provide safe play spaces and appropriate equipment at the right age. She welcomes your help when she tackles a new task, from pulling up on to her feet to taking those historic first steps. When she falters, your sympathy and encouragement can dis-spell momentary feelings of failure; and when she's successful, how she loves your praise! She welcomes the variety you can devise—new things to crawl through, to climb over, to slide down, to swat. Last but far from least, she likes playing all kinds of games with you. This chapter helps all of you enjoy active play and exercise.

LOVING TOUCHES

Touching and stroking are a form of communication. A baby picks up unspoken messages about adults from the way they handle her, in much the same way that we form impressions of people based on

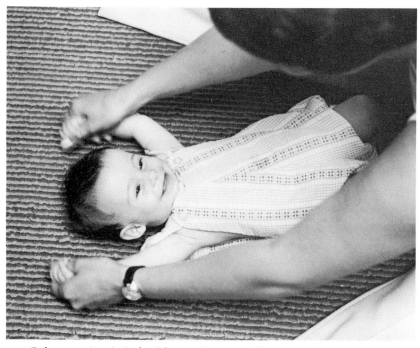

Baby exercises help build muscles, co-ordinate movements – and
they're *fun*!

handshakes and embraces. Expressing your love through caring touch
gives your baby a sense of security.

Most babies enjoy physical stimulation right from birth. A baby
also *needs* a certain amount of touching, cuddling and rocking for
proper development. In the past, some institutionally raised children
received proper food and other physical care but were rarely held. They
often failed to thrive. You needn't worry about that, however. Your
baby typically receives lots of physical stimulation during feeding
(when she's held and rocked), bathing and dressing, and when you
cuddle her and soothe her cries. If you're brand-new parents, though,
with all the things new parents think and worry about, you might
overlook ways to add variety to these regular routines. Two very
pleasant ways are massages and exercises.

Individual Differences

Babies differ in how much they like to be held and cuddled. Most
welcome the close, secure contact, but some chafe at the seeming
restraint unless very sleepy. Some babies, too, don't especially like to

be stroked and massaged. If your baby isn't a cuddler, don't take it as a sign of personal rejection; it's just part of the personal style she was born with. She might prefer being rocked in a cradle.

Baby Exercises

Even though your baby can't move her limbs with co-ordination, *you* can, with simple baby exercises. When she's on her stomach, hold her feet and help her to do some frog kicks: up (heels touch her bottom), out (legs straightened in a 'V'), and back together. On her back you can bicycle her legs and stretch her arms.

Many parents and babies I know have developed their own set of baby exercise routines – and each is unique to them. The following simple exercises, best introduced after 1 month, will get you started. Make up more!

1. Bring your baby's hands together, cross them over her chest, then stretch them out to the sides.
2. Stretch both arms up past her head, then down to her sides.
3. Stretch one arm up, the other down, then alternate.
4. Do some knee bends: both legs together, or one leg, then the other.
5. Touch your baby's left hand to her right knee, then alternate.

Play Tips

o Repeat a single exercise any number of times, then switch to another. Combine a series of separate exercises into a continuous routine.

o Exercise on a soft surface.

o Keep your movements gentle and smooth. Never jerk your baby into position. Let her set the pace, too, by watching her cues and reactions. Some babies like quiet exercising, others more rigorous routines.

o Sing or chant favourite nursery rhymes (or popular songs), and move your baby to the rhythm.

Stroking and Massaging

End bathtime or a nappy change with a soothing massage. Gently and rhythmically rub or stroke your baby's back, stomach and limbs. Use your bare hands, or add variety by wearing a soft glove or mitten. You might also try stroking your baby with a very soft artist's paintbrush, a large feather, or a cotton wool ball. Always watch her reaction to see whether she's enjoying these different sensations.

I recommend that you ask your health visitor before massaging your baby with lotion or baby oil. Some babies have naturally oily skin and shouldn't have the additional moisture. Also, a young baby's pores often don't work properly (one reason she may get prickly heat in warm weather), and the lotion may clog them.

——————— KICKING GAMES ———————

By about 4 months, your baby can control her leg movements and loves to flail around and kick up her heels. Turn this into a fun exercise with the following game:

o Your baby lies on her back – in her cot, in the middle of your bed, or on a mat on the floor. You dangle a large toy over her feet, encouraging her to give it some spirited kicks. Use an easy-to-hit target that swings and makes sounds – these rewards encourage her to keep on kicking. You could tap the toy against her feet a few times to start her off.

The perfect toy? A big rattle, a foam-filled fabric cube with a bell inside (stitch on a piece of elastic or ribbon to dangle it by), or this Super Kicker. It's big, it swings, it makes sounds.

SUPER KICKER

Ideal Intro Age: 4 months
Age Range: 4 to 8 months
FOR SUPERVISED PLAY ONLY

Tools and Materials

☆ Empty cereal box, with the lining (and crumbs) removed

☆ Piece of thick wool or ribbon, about 60 cm (24 in) long

☆ Scissors, knife, or large nail (for punching holes)

☆ Jingle bells, small rattles, dried beans, or other small soundmakers

☆ Tape

Instructions

1. Drop the soundmakers into the clean, empty box.
2. Punch a hole in each narrow side, near the top.
3. Thread the wool or ribbon through both holes and tie the ends together to form a loop.
4. Tape the lid securely shut.

SAFETY NOTE: For supervised play only. If left alone, your baby might try to pick off – and eat – the tape. Also, if she should get the box open, she might try to swallow the soundmakers.

A great toy for spirited kicking fun – the homemade Super Kicker.

At 3 or 4 months old, babies enjoy being pulled up to a sitting position.

BEGINNING TO SIT

Babies go through several stages in learning to sit up. At about 3 or 4 months, when they easily control the muscles supporting the head, most babies enjoy sitting while supported on a parent's lap or in a swing or other seat. They also enjoy being pulled to the sitting position, in junior versions of sit-ups:

o   Lay your baby on her back on a smooth surface (the cot mattress, your bed, your lap, etc.).

o   Grasp her hands and s-l-o-w-l-y pull her to the sitting position. Hold tight so she doesn't fall.

o   Gently lower her again.

At first her back may sag and her head may lag behind her shoulders, but as her muscles strengthen she sags less and less. In fact, between about 5 and 6 months she might grab your extended hands and pull *herself* up.

At around 6 months most babies can sit with minimal support – perhaps with a small pillow behind the back or with just one hand held to aid their balance. When sitting, too, a baby might lean forward and support her weight on her outstretched arms. Within a month or so most babies sit fully upright.

More ways to help:

○ When your baby begins sitting alone, let her practise on a soft surface or surround her with pillows. These cushion her temporary tumbles and reduce discouragement.

○ Once she's up, the novice sitter might not be able to get out of the sitting position without help. A slumping back or an unhappy face might tell you that she's ready to return to lying on her stomach or back, or wants you to pick her up.

TOYS AND GAMES FOR THE CRAWLER

Crawling is a giant stride towards independence. Once your baby begins scooting around under her own power, usually between 8 and 10 months, she need no longer depend totally on others to choose her play spaces and materials. She helps decide where she wants to go and what she wants to explore. Freedom! But with it comes responsibility – your responsibility for making the home safe for her excursions.

SAFETY NOTE: Now that your baby is crawling it's time to baby-proof your home. Check out the suggestions in good child care books.

| The Royal Society for the Prevention of Accidents publishes a helpful safety pamphlet called *The Home Safety Book*. You can order a copy (price 50p) from: | Sales Department, ROSPA, Cannon House, Priory Queensway, Birmingham B4 6BS *Tel.* 021-200 2461 |

Your baby has been preparing for crawling all this year; you've helped with massages, exercises, all types of general large-muscle play. Now that she seems ready for this new milestone, give her some extra practice. Make sure she has plenty of chances to flail about stomach-down on a firm surface. Placing your hands against the soles of her feet, so she has something to push against, might give her the traction she needs to get started.

Add encouragement at the front end, too. For instance, offer a favourite toy or delectable finger food for her to crawl to and capture; or invite her to crawl into your outstretched arms.

Once your baby starts crawling fairly well, she needs no encouragement other than the thrill of moving about under her own power. (In fact, at times you'll wish that she weren't so self-driving!) But after mastering the rudiments, she probably likes the additional challenge of these games and toys.

Bear in mind that babies move forwards in many different ways – rolling, creeping, pulling themselves along with their hands while sitting, slithering like a snake. Not all babies use the conventional hands-and-knees method of crawling.

Simple Games

○ Drag a pull-along toy slowly across the floor for your baby to pursue. Make sure she catches it after a time. Is she getting quite speedy? Pull it faster.

○ Roll a ball and invite her to 'Go and get it.'

○ Get down on the floor and let her chase *you*. 'Ah – you've got me!'

Floor Pillows

Big, soft pillows are wonderful for active play like pounding on or crawling over, or quiet times like nestling into for a brief rest or sharing a picture book with you. Let your baby play on the floor with your bed pillows. Or make her a T-shirt Pillow of her very own. If you have time, make several; different sizes can have different functions. Your baby can flop on or roll or crawl over a large pillow on the floor. A group of medium-sized pillows double as soft building boulders. Your older toddler might also use them in a gentle pillow fight (the sleeves are easy hand-holds). Still smaller pillows can be thrown and caught. Pillows with cheerful patterns make unique room decorations.

SAFETY NOTE: Never leave a young baby unsupervised on a pillow, or use a pillow in the cot, because of the risk of suffocation.

T-SHIRT PILLOW

Ideal Intro Age: 9 months
Age Range: 9 to 36 months

Tools and Materials

☆ T-shirt with a colourful design

☆ Stuffing material, such as polyester fibrefill or shredded foam; make sure it's machine washable and dryer safe

☆ Sewing machine or needle and thread

Instructions

1. Sew closed the sleeve holes and neck.
2. Stuff the shirt tightly through the open bottom and then sew closed.

HINT: For a deluxe (albeit more time-consuming) version, sew patches of different-textured fabrics on to the T-shirt before stuffing. Your baby likes exploring these varied surfaces. Make sure all the patches are securely attached and that the fabrics are machine washable.

A homemade T-shirt Pillow is terrific for crawling over or nestling into.

Tunnels for Crawling Through

Tunnels are mysterious and exciting. For your baby, crawling through a tunnel is a form of peekaboo – she disappears, then reappears like magic. The tunnel itself is a cosy sort of temporary hideout. Older babies and toddlers like having their own territory in the larger adult environment.

Any piece of furniture under which she fits can be a tunnel, be it coffee table or dining room chair. You can even make a tunnel from a large cardboard carton. Tape shut the top flaps and cut tunnel-shaped openings in any two opposing sides. Make sure you leave some 'framing' around the tunnel openings – this gives the box stability. Alternatively, make the soft-textured Fuzzy Crawl-through below.

Tunnel Games

o Put a toy at one end of the tunnel for your baby to crawl towards and retrieve.

o Play Follow the Leader: you crawl through the tunnel first (if you can fit); your baby follows. Or an older brother or sister can lead.

o A tunnel can be part of the Indoor Obstacle Course (page 92).

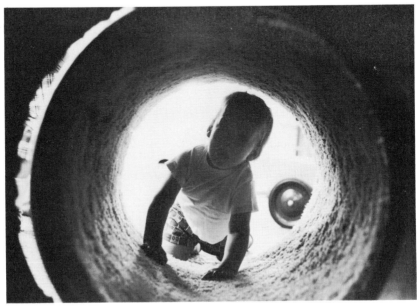

The Fuzzy Crawl-through adds delightful texture to all-fours trips.

FUZZY CRAWL-THROUGH

Ideal Intro Age: 10 months
Age Range: 10 to 24 months

Tools and Materials

☆ Carpet remnant, about 2×1 m (6×3 ft); it must have a fairly stiff backing

☆ Strong tape – carpet tape or reinforced wrapping tape

Instructions

1. Roll the carpet lengthwise into a cylinder, with the backing side out.
2. Secure with two or three bands of tape stretched around the circumference of the rolled carpet.

HINT: You might also try a tunnel with a different diameter. Remember that the diameter of a circle is roughly one-third of its circumference (distance around). Thus, a 2-m (6-ft) piece of carpet, when rolled, creates a tunnel about 60 cm (2 ft) in diameter.

Play Tips

○ For a different sort of exercise, lay your baby across the outside of the carpet tunnel, hold her firmly by the waist or thighs, and gently roll her back and forth.
○ Stand the tunnel on end – it makes a great place to store balls and large toys. An older toddler might also like using it as a giant container for throwing balls and stuffed toys into. Then she can push it over – *crash!* – to retrieve them.

Obstacle Course

Combine several things to crawl over, under, around and through into a baby-sized obstacle course.

INDOOR OBSTACLE COURSE

Ideal Intro Age: 10 months
Age Range: 10 to 18 months

Tools and Materials

☆ Simple obstacles for your baby to crawl over, under, around and through. Some suggestions:

○ Large T-shirt Pillow (page 89)

○ Fuzzy Crawl-through (page 91)

○ Firm chair or sofa cushions

○ Plain cardboard boxes

○ Dining room chair (without rods between the legs), for crawling under

○ Giant stuffed animals

Instructions

1. Scatter some obstacles around the floor.
2. Encourage your baby to crawl from one to another, following a 'course'. Over this pillow. Around this box. Under this chair. Through this tunnel. Big hugs and applause for completing manoeuvres!

Play Tips

○ Try some Follow the Leader. You lead the way around the course; your baby follows. This game is usually a good one for an older brother or sister to play with baby.
○ Chase the Toy: this time a favourite toy leads the way. You shake it beside each obstacle; your baby scoots around trying to catch it. Be sure to give her the prize if she seems to be getting frustrated by the elusive chase.

— UP WE GO —

Soon after your baby learns to crawl she begins climbing. Now she's magically drawn to the staircase. Remember: it's unsafe! The padded steps of Climb and Slide are better and also form the base for a slide.

CLIMB AND SLIDE

Ideal Intro Age: 12 months
Age Range: 12 to 18 months
FOR SUPERVISED PLAY ONLY
(see page 94)

Tools and Materials

☆ Several firm sofa or chair   ☆ Large cardboard box
  seat cushions

Instructions

1. For climbing: build a series of broad steps with the cushions.
2. For sliding: cut open the cardboard box to make a long runway. Be sure it has no staples or rough edges. Lay it on top of the cushion steps.

SAFETY NOTE: Because your crawler is so keen to climb, it's time to put a safety gate across the stairs. Block both the top and the bottom.

Play Tips

○ For climbing: your toddler starts at the bottom of the steps; you're at the top. Encourage her to crawl up and get the prize (a toy, a big hug). Make sure she doesn't tumble off the side.
○ For sliding: initially it's best if both parents take part. One stands at the top and holds the cardboard to prevent it sliding forwards. The other holds your toddler by waist or legs and helps her slide down to the bottom. When she sits quite confidently and slides well, let her try it without being held.

Build this homemade Climb and Slide to challenge the crawler. Cover it with a large sheet of cardboard to make a first slide.

FIRST STEPS

Now the truly big achievement – walking. Even before your baby takes those all-important first steps, usually between 10 and 15 months, she's been pulling herself to a standing position by holding a support, like the cot or playpen rail, or the sofa. For walking practice she probably cruises from one end of the sofa to the other, moving hand-over-hand, or around the coffee table (be sure it hasn't a sharp edge). These trial excursions strengthen her legs and help her learn to balance while standing. You can help, too, by walking with her, holding one or both of her hands.

Does she seem ready to join the upright race? Stand her on the floor. When she's steady on her feet, let go, move back a few steps, and call to her with outstretched arms: 'Come on, Eleanor, come to Daddy. Good for you, Eleanor!'

Like crawling, walking is its own reward. Yet also like crawling, there are games and toys that make it more fun:

The new walker loves being a go-between from parent to parent.

○ Both parents sit a short distance apart on the floor. Send your toddler back and forth, like a go-between. She might carry a 'present' (a toy) from parent to parent. Reward her crossings with thanks and hugs.

○ Take frequent strolls outside. The terrain of hard, flat pavement and gently rolling lawn is quite different from floor and carpet.

○ Try more games of chase. You hobble away on hands and knees; your toddler pursues on two legs. Make sure she catches you.

○ Since the skilled walker often likes to carry something, invite her to be your special messenger. She might bring you something (unbreakable!) from the coffee table or bookshelf, or help you carry the washing, or bring an item (box of cereal) in from the car after a shopping trip.

Pull and Push Toys

The experienced walker also likes dragging a pull-along toy about as she walks. The best ones make sounds so that your child is sure the toy is still following her without having to turn around to look. A pull-along toy with parts that can be shaken, rolled, and fitted or stacked on to the base offers many added play opportunities.

Starting at around 18 months or so, toddlers also like push-along toys with rigid handles. These, too, are more fun if they make sounds and spin or otherwise move as your child pushes them. Currently popular are plastic lawn mowers, wheelbarrows and vacuum cleaners, since these have built-in imitation appeal.

RAMP GAMES

If your toddler loves balls and toys that roll (and most toddlers do), add novelty to her play with some ramp games. They're fun ways to practise eye–hand and locomotion skills. First, though, you need to create a ramp (see opposite).

Here are some suggestions for ramp games:

○ Simplest: you roll a toy down the ramp, it races across the floor, and your toddler chases after it and brings it back to you.

○ Your toddler rolls the toy down the ramp and you chase it.

○ Each of you holds a rolling toy at the top of the ramp. Ready – steady – *go!* Release your toys. Down they roll ... across the floor they zoom.

Ramps add drama, excitement, lots of skill-building exercise.

RAMPS FOR ROLLER GAMES

Ideal Intro Age: 15 months
Age Range: 12 to 36 months
FOR SUPERVISED PLAY ONLY

Tools and Materials

☆ Ramp – any broad plank that's at least 30 cm (12 in) long (longer, if possible) and about 23–30 cm (9–12 in) wide. Some suggestions:

○ Extra shelf from the bookcase

○ Large cutting board or pastry board

○ Long, flat gift box

○ Spare piece of wood or plank bought at a timber merchant or DIY store; make sure it has no splinters or sharp edges

☆ Support – some suggestions:

○ Sofa cushions

○ Stack of books

○ Cardboard box

○ Cardboard Block (page 69)

Instructions

Rest one end of the ramp on the support.

HINT: The shorter the ramp and higher the support, the faster the toy rolls.

Whose went fastest? Farthest? Good game for brothers and sisters! See who can retrieve her toy and bring it back to the top of the ramp first.

○ You let go of the toy and your toddler tries to catch it at the bottom of the ramp. (Best if you use a long, sloping ramp.)

○ Ramp bowling: set up pins at the bottom for your toddler to knock over with her rolling toy. Try plastic tumblers, tall wooden bricks, empty plastic bottles.

SAFETY NOTE: You should supervise these games, because left alone your toddler might try to walk up or slide down the ramp. Most of these homemade versions won't support her weight.

———————— TERRIFIC TUBES ————————

Large mailing tubes and rolling toys small enough to fit inside create dramatic play possibilities for the toddler who is 15 months and older. You can probably buy tubes at the stationers. Cut off both ends. Tennis balls are great for these games. So are transparent balls with spinners inside:

○ You drop the ball into the tube; your toddler chases it when it emerges.

○ You hold the tube; your toddler drops the ball inside and chases it.

○ You hold one end of the tube; your toddler holds the other. Put a ball into the tube and roll it back and forth by tilting the tube.

○ When your toddler plays alone: tape or tie a tube to the outside of a table or playpen, slanting down and low enough for your toddler to reach easily. For a change of game, place a basket on the floor under the tube to catch the balls.

HINT: Cardboard tubes, all sizes, are fun even without the rolling toys. Peek at each other through a short tube (from an empty roll of paper towels, perhaps), or whisper to each other. Longer, stronger tubes make fine toddler rounders bats. Your child will find plenty of other uses, too.

SAFETY NOTE: A reminder . . . ping-pong balls are too small. Your toddler might get one lodged in her throat.

A large mailing tube and some rolling toys offer great play possibilities.

—— BRIDGES AND BALANCE BEAMS ——

Another challenge for the steady walker is a low bridge to walk across. This is often called a balance beam, although on a real one the surface is narrow; for this age it must be wide. You can make a temporary version by resting a broad plank on two boxes, or even on the bars between the legs of two chairs. Always supervise, though, because the plank might easily move about. Also, hold your toddler's hand for early crossings.

NOTE: Some toddlers hesitate about walking a balance beam, whereas others take to it immediately. If your child baulks, it's better not to force her.

This homemade Balance Bridge is a more permanent version. When your child is older, it will also probably inspire all sorts of fantasy play (the drawbridge over a castle moat, for example, or perhaps the bridge in the *Three Billy Goats Gruff*).

BALANCE BRIDGE

Ideal Intro Age: 15 months
Age Range: 15 to 36 months

Tools and Materials

☆ Wooden plank or shelf, about 30 cm (12 in) wide and 60–90 cm (24–36 in) long

☆ 2 cardboard boxes, at least 30 cm (12 in) long and wide, and about 15 cm (6 in) high

☆ Newspaper

☆ Strong packing or wrapping tape

Instructions

1. Stuff each box completely full with wadded newspaper and tape it closed. The paper adds strength.
2. Tape a box on each end of the plank. Use two bands of tape per box, and run each band across the plank and all the way around the box, as shown.

RIDING TOYS

Most parents I've interviewed introduce a riding toy when their child is just about 12 months old. This seems to be a good age, as long as you're aware of just how the new toddler uses it.

From 12 to about 15 months, toddlers don't ride a toy in the conventional sense. Rather, they get on and off. And on and off. They use it as a perch from which to observe their surroundings. They sit on it and push *backwards*. They get off and push it across the floor. They sit on it.

From about 15 months toddlers begin pushing themselves forwards on a riding toy. They also turn it upside down and play with the wheels. At these young ages, a toddler is usually unable to steer it accurately or use pedals. But she does like to be pushed.

Steering usually comes in between 18 and 24 months, pedalling a bit later. So we can say there are two phases of riding toys, with an appropriate type for each:

○ 12 to 18 months, when ride-ons should be simple, without pedals, and non-steerable (although if the toy does have steering, it isn't automatically a drawback — just not a necessity).

○ 18 months onwards, when toys should offer steering and pedalling, even though these features (especially the pedals) might get little use for the first few months.

When Choosing a Ride-on

You'll find a staggering array of riding toys on the market. The following guidelines might help you choose the best for your child. No one toy will have all these features, so decide which you think are most important. Also, take your toddler with you when making your selection, to ensure that she can handle the particular toy; that is, get on and off unaided, manage the steering, and so forth.

Favourite Ride-on Features

○ Easy mount/dismount. Make sure your toddler can get on and off all by herself, otherwise she'll cry for your help — and you won't always be able to comply. Also remember that younger toddlers tend to 'walk onto' a riding toy from the back: they aren't yet able to swing their leg over the seat.

o Covered storage compartment that you can easily clean. All kinds of things – dirt, twigs, food – will find their way inside.

o A contoured seat that cradles your toddler, so that she doesn't slide off backwards. However, be sure that the backrest isn't so high that it hampers her ability to get on and off.

o A horn, bell, or other soundmaker that she can work.

o Concealed wheels, or a wheelbase that's long enough so your toddler doesn't bump the front wheels with her toes. Remember: at first she pushes herself backwards.

o Stability. A ride-on shouldn't easily tip forwards, backwards or sideways. To test a steering toy, turn the wheels all the way to one side and give a tug forwards. If it tips readily, look for one with better balance.

o Stability when turned upside down. This is a popular way for toddlers to play with their ride-ons.

o Additional features, like a telephone, toys to fit on to the ride-on, a workbench, or the like.

o For you: a ride-on should be compact enough for easy storage, light enough to carry from indoors to outdoors or from room to room, and easy to wash.

—— JUMPING AND BOUNCING FUN ——

'Stop bouncing on the bed!' thundered Daddy from downstairs as the chandelier swung madly over the dining room table.

'You'll break it – or your neck,' Mummy called up the staircase in chorus.

Remember something like that? Well, with this Toddler Trampoline, your young child can jump, roll, flop and flounder to her heart's content – sparing furniture from destruction. It's best for homes with plenty of toddler play space, since it takes up a lot of room.

This homemade Toddler Trampoline was a great success in schools; you can make your own.

TODDLER TRAMPOLINE

Ideal Intro Age: 18 months
Age Range: 15 to 36 months

Tools and Materials

☆ Single-bed mattress (or even the cot mattress)

☆ Fitted sheet

Instructions

Put the sheet on the mattress, the mattress on the floor.

HINTS: Since the mattress is for active play rather than sleeping on, its condition doesn't matter as long as the cover isn't ripped. Also, if space is a problem, you can store the trampoline under a bed during non-playtimes.

SAFETY NOTE: Although most toddlers can't really bounce like circus tumblers, it's safest to position the trampoline some distance from any wall when your child uses it unsupervised.

Play Tips

○ Initially your toddler will probably like just walking around on her Toddler Trampoline – it's not firm like the floor or garden path. She'll gradually work up to falling and flopping and jumping. Jumping is especially fun when you hold her hands, or hold her under her arms and bounce her up and down.

○ Put some lively music on the radio or stereo.

———— TODDLER BALL GAMES ————

As a single item, a ball is probably the most indispensable toy for active play. It can be rolled, bounced, thrown, caught, kicked, whacked with a stick, dropped through a hoop, chased after – and that's just the beginning. Collect a variety of balls for your toddler. Different balls lend themselves to different types of play, depending on their size and material. Different children play with balls in different ways, too, depending on the *child's* size and interests. Here are some games and ideas to get you started:

○ Sit on the floor, a short distance away from your toddler, and roll a ball back and forth. Your toddler's aim might be a bit off, but she'll have fun trying, and fun exchanging this object between you.

○ Safe throwing: use a rolled-up pair of socks as a ball. Ask your toddler to throw it to you. She'll probably throw it anywhere – even behind her – but the soft socks won't damage anything. With lots of practice she'll improve her aim.

Balls inspire so many kinds of play; they're indispensable active toys.

○ Inflated beach balls are a special treat because they're so large (and therefore look 'heavy' to a toddler), but they are light enough for her to carry easily. Bounce a beach ball on her head. Roll it back and forth between you two (or three or more). Hold your toddler under her arms so she's standing, and then swing her lightly back and forth making her 'kick' the ball.

○ Balloons, too, are magical balls. Sit facing each other and bat a balloon back and forth; or demonstrate how batting a balloon by oneself keeps it aloft; or drop a balloon for your toddler to catch.

SAFETY NOTE: Always supervise her play with balloons. If one should pop, she might choke on the limp rubber. See also the Hand Paddles (page 110).

○ Near 24 months, your toddler might be able to catch a ball thrown to her. Usually, she'll stretch out both arms, catch the ball between them, then cradle it and draw it to her chest. Ask her to try throwing it back.

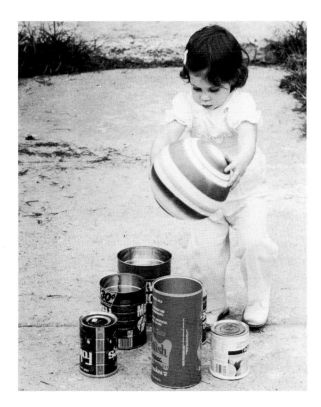

Junior bowling!

○ At this age she can probably also kick a ball if you hold her hand for balance. Alone she might walk into the ball rather than kick it conventionally. True kicking is hard; it requires balancing on one foot while swinging the other.

○ A large rubber ball and several coffee tins make a nice clangy bowling set. Show how to roll the ball and knock the tins down. Then let your toddler try. Set up the tins again after she bowls them over. Don't be surprised if she devises her own way of playing. Some toddlers, rather than rolling the ball, carry it up to the tins and knock them over; some throw the ball; some carry the ball and kick the tins over.

To help ensure success, create an alley that prevents the ball from straying off course. The sides can be made from sofa cushions or cardboard boxes. Try outdoor bowling, too.

—ARM GAMES FOR OLDER TODDLERS—

Pulling Punches

Is your toddler momentarily angry or frustrated? A few rounds at a punching bag can help work off some aggression.

A punching bag fits into less pugnacious times, too. Hitting a hanging bag is a good way for your toddler to exercise her arms and practise eye–hand co-ordination. (From her point of view, though, it's merely a fun way to play.) This indoor Punching Bag is perfect.

PUNCHING BAG

Ideal Intro Age: 18 months
Age Range: 18 to 36 months
BEST FOR SUPERVISED PLAY: see SAFETY NOTE opposite
(see page 108)

Tools and Materials

☆ Old pair of adult-sized blue jeans (or other trousers)

☆ Newspaper, about 20 or more double-page sheets

☆ Sewing machine or needle and thread

☆ Piece of strong rope, about 1.5 m (5 ft) long

☆ Hammer

☆ Large nail or hook

▶

Instructions

1. Cut off one leg from the jeans, turn this leg inside out, and sew up the cut end.
2. Turn right-side-out again and stuff about three-quarters full with crumpled newspaper.
3. Tie closed the opening with one end of the rope. Make the knot *tight*.
4. Tie a small loop at the other end of the rope, and hang the bag in the centre of an open doorway, slipping the loop over a strong nail or sturdy hook driven into the door frame. The bottom of the bag should be about 30–60 cm (1–2 ft) off the floor.

HINT: Save the remainder of the jeans for making the Blue Jeans Bag (page 177).

SAFETY NOTE: This is best for supervised play, because on her own your toddler may swing on the bag, which could be dangerous: one, it might come crashing down under her weight; two, she might swing into the side of the door frame. Slip the bag off the nail when playtime's over. It's probably safer if your child doesn't play alone with this toy even when it's not hanging from a support. There's a slight chance that she might get tangled in the rope and choke.

Play Tips

o Your beginning puncher might be more confident if you hold the bag still as she hits it.

o Add some early learning about numbers by counting aloud each time your toddler punches the bag.

o Put some bouncy music on the radio or stereo to accompany your child's workout.

o Hang the bag outside, from a low tree branch, and let your older toddler (over 24 months) swat it with a child-sized plastic cricket bat or plastic tennis racquet, or even a sturdy cardboard tube.

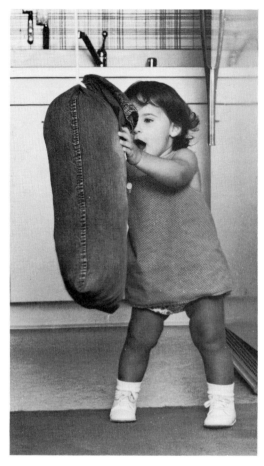

A homemade Punching Bag
thrills any young pugilist.

Throwing Game

Here's another standby from our own childhood — throwing a ball,
beanbag, or other object at a target.

Bear in mind that hitting a target isn't as simple as you might
think. First, your toddler has to understand the point of the game —
hitting the target with the thrown toy. Second, she must have the
ability to let go of the toy at will, and the co-ordination to aim her
throws. These are developed with time and practice. In the early
stages, therefore, your child might stand right by the target and just
drop the ammo into the box, or hit the ammo against the target and
then place it in the box. That's fine — this game has no real rules.

The Target Practice toy illustrated opposite gives ideas for good
targets to create and for appropriate ammunition.

TARGET PRACTICE

Ideal Intro Age: 24 months
Age Range: 24 to 36 months

Tools and Materials

☆ Target:

○ Large piece of paper or posterboard

○ Crayons or felt-tipped markers

○ Masking tape, at least 2.5 cm (1 in) wide

☆ Basket or shallow box

☆ Ammunition – anything your toddler can throw easily:

○ Beanbags (see Sock Beanbags, page 61)

○ Small stuffed animals

○ Plastic bricks

Instructions

1. Draw a colourful target on the paper or posterboard. Some suggestions:

○ Silly animal face with huge open mouth

○ Pair of outstretched hands

○ Bull's-eye of differently coloured rings

○ Colourful clown

2. Tape the target on to a wall and place the box or basket underneath to catch the thrown ammo (and store it in between playtimes).

Play Tips

○ Count each object as your toddler throws it – good for early number learning.

○ Take turns aiming at the target. Your older child might like to play, too.

○ If the target is an animal face with gaping jaws, you can pretend that the ammo is food, and you and your toddler are tossing titbits to the hungry beast. Beanbags, with their amorphous shape, are good for this version: 'And here's another fish for Stella Seal.'

○ If the target is a clown or other face, pretend he's a bad actor and you're pelting him with rotten tomatoes: 'Boo! Hiss!'

HAND PADDLES

Ideal Intro Age: 24 months
Age Range: 24 to 36 months

Tools and Materials

☆ Paper plate, dinner-sized; choose the rigid moulded type with a rim, as an ordinary paper plate is too flimsy

☆ Elastic, 2.5 cm (1 in) wide and about 25 cm (10 in) long

☆ Knife

☆ Needle and thread

FRONT

BACK

Instructions

1. Make two slits, about 12.5 cm (5 in) apart, in the plate. Each should be a little more than 2.5 cm (1 in) long.
2. Thread the elastic through both slits, then sew the elastic ends together, pulling up any slack.
3. To wear the paddle, slip a hand between the elastic and the bottom of the plate.

Play Tips

o Give your toddler a Hand Paddle and a balloon. How many times can she bat the balloon into the air without letting it touch the ground? Count each hit aloud, too, for number learning.

o You and your toddler (or toddler and another child) each wear a paddle and hit the balloon back and forth.

o Crumple a sheet of newspaper into a ball, then run clear adhesive tape or masking tape around the outside to hold its shape. You throw this ball and your toddler smacks it with her Hand Paddle.

o Create a newspaper ball, tape on a piece of string, and hang the ball outdoors from a clothesline, low branch, or other support. Your toddler can swat it.

SAFETY NOTE: Supervise your toddler's play with a balloon. It could frighten her if it pops, and if she put the limp rubber into her mouth she might choke on it.

Throw a wadded newspaper
ball for your toddler to
smack with her homemade
Hand Paddle.

More Ball Games

Many older toddlers like to swat a ball or balloon with their hands. The
trouble is, they sometimes lack the co-ordination to hit accurately.
Because a homemade Hand Paddle 'makes' your child's hand much
larger, it helps ensure success.

———————— WATER SLIDE ————————

A slippery, slidy sheet of wet plastic on the lawn is the perfect cooler on
hot summer days – for your toddler, her friends and older brothers and
sisters, even you if you want to join in the fun. This Slippery Slider is
not only delightful, it's great exercise to boot.

SLIPPERY SLIDER

Ideal Intro Age: 24 months
Age Range: 18 to 36 months
FOR SUPERVISED PLAY ONLY

Tools and Materials

☆ *Heavy-gauge* plastic tarpaulin or painting dustsheet. (Thin plastic will *not* stand up to the vigorous play this toy gets. Also, it might suffocate a child if misused.) Heavy plastic tarpaulins can be found at hardware shops, DIY shops, most shops that sell housepaint, and camping supply centres

☆ Lawn sprinkler

Instructions

1. Spread the tarpaulin flat over a patch of lawn – *not* a bare spot of ground (it'll get muddy), and *not* a driveway or other hard surface. Be sure the area beneath is free of stones, rocks, branches, and other hard objects that might rip the plastic or injure a child as she slides.
2. Position the sprinkler near one end of the tarpaulin and turn on the water. When the tarpaulin's completely wet, start playing!

HINTS: Keep the water running as long as you play. Also, move the slide around occasionally so that the grass underneath doesn't smother, or become too waterlogged, or get cooked by the hot sun penetrating through the plastic.

SAFETY NOTE: *Always* supervise a young child when she's in or around water. There's always a chance of drowning – and the younger she is, the greater the chance. Even with the Slippery Slider, she could possibly inhale some water.

Play Tips

o Play speedboat: grab your toddler's ankles and push her around the wet surface of the Slippery Slider while she lies on her stomach.

o Play 'the old man and the sea': you're the fisherman and your toddler is the prize fish. She grabs the end of a rope while lying on her stomach and you pull her around the Slider.

o Does your child enjoy fantasy play? Ask her to pretend she's a whale . . . a goldfish . . . a sea horse. . . . Or you can both pretend you're sea creatures and act out an underwater adventure.

o Great toy for older children to use, too. Make sure they don't become too boisterous around your toddler.

Beat the heat with a homemade Slippery Slider.

TO SUM UP

Just think! In three short years your child has changed from a tiny curled-up newborn into a confident toddler who runs and jumps and climbs. But physical skill is only one part of her marvellous self. Let's look next at language.

language fun 5

'W-a-a-a-a-a-a-h-h-h-h-h!'

'O-o-o-o-o-o-o-o-o.'

'Babadabadadawawawababa.'

'Ma ma!'

'Doggie!'

'Daddy car.'

'Juice all gone.'

Learning to talk, like any other skill, is a process that begins at birth and proceeds in a continuous pattern throughout the early years. Like other skills, too, language learning has several important milestones, as illustrated in the examples above: crying, cooing vowel sounds, babbling, first words, early sentences, and the like. These unfold according to each child's inner developmental timetable. You don't really teach your baby to talk, just as you don't teach him to sit up or walk; but there are lots of ways to enhance your child's language skills through play.

—————DEVELOPMENTAL SUMMARY—————

Talking is such a complicated process that it would take thousands of pages to describe all the intricate steps. Bear that in mind as you read this drastically abbreviated summary of some important highlights. Also remember that the ages given are averages. Almost no baby follows this pattern to a T. In addition, since most of the research has been done with babies and mothers (rather than fathers), findings don't mention fathers very often.

Birth to About 3 Months

At birth a baby is primed for communication. He prefers human speech (especially his mother's) to any other sounds, and listens to speech in a special way. Within a few weeks a baby and mother develop a sort of prototype conversation. As the mother speaks, the baby moves his face, lips and tongue, arms and hands, and even whole body in time with her voice. For example, when the mother pauses, the baby moves as if it's his turn to 'speak'.

From a very young age a baby can tell the difference between similar speech sounds; for instance, *pa* and *ba*. Recognizing such differences is the foundation of understanding any language.

The newborn's first 'word' is his cry, and over the early weeks cries form a symbolic language. Some say 'I'm hungry'. Some say 'I'm bored'. Some call urgently with an 'I need you!' intensity. Parents pick up these differences almost instinctively. When you respond to cries you are teaching your baby something else about language — that his voice attracts attention. This is another early form of conversation.

By about 6 weeks a baby conveys feelings with sounds other than cries, and by 3 months he coos and gurgles and squeals with pleasure.

Talking to your baby is the very best way to build language skills.

3 to About 6 Months

A baby of this age experiments with making various sounds. He chuckles and laughs, gurgles and squeals, growls, grunts, and blows bubbles with saliva. He may vocalize tunefully or make long 'speeches' when looking at people or things that interest him. By the age of 6 months he usually makes both single and double syllables — for example, *ka, muh, adah, erleh*.

His understanding of words is likewise growing. In familiar mother–baby games he may make appropriate gestures to key words, such as trying to clap his hands as you recite Pat-a-cake. Or when you accompany certain words in a familiar rhyme with tickling, he may begin to laugh at the words alone, anticipating the tickle.

6 to About 9 Months

A baby of this age can identify different harmonic patterns in the way sentences are spoken. Questions have rising tunes, statements have falling tunes. Exclamations, like 'What a shock you gave me!', have a different tune altogether. He also understands simple commands like 'No, no' and 'Bye-bye', and responds when called by name. He uses easily understood gestures as well to make his feelings known, such as waving away unwanted food or shaking his head when he doesn't want to do something.

The sounds he makes are becoming more like true speech. At first he makes consonant-vowel sounds like *ma, pa, da, di, wa*, which use primarily the lips. Initially he makes such sounds one at a time, but soon he strings them into rhythmic babbles — *babababababababa*. Later he adds more difficult sounds — *s, f* and *ts* (as in *cats*) — although, interestingly, these sounds rarely appear in first words. He uses his voice to make his feelings known and to get things he wants. He shouts for attention, or tries to make contact with another person with a cough or other noise. In a sense, we can say he vocalizes deliberately as a means of communication.

9 to About 12 Months

Babbling peaks during this age. Babies make long, tuneful utterances that sound very much like real sentences if you don't listen too closely. They make different sounds to indicate different wants and needs.

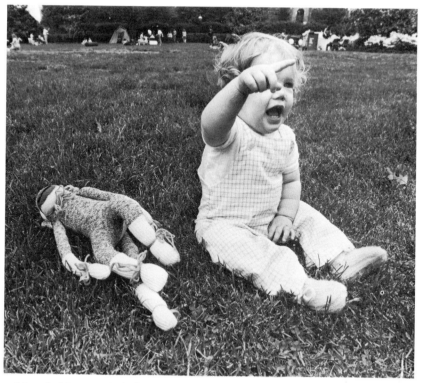

Most babies say their first real word between 10 and about 13 months.

These can usually be interpreted correctly by parents and people close to the baby, but may mystify casual acquaintances. Near the end of this period (usually between 10 and 13 months), a baby says his first word that is generally understandable to almost everyone.

But well before this time, your baby understands many things said to him. Word comprehension always precedes and outpaces word production. At this age he knows his own name and the names of other familiar people. He understands and acts on simple commands like 'Come here' and 'Show me your nose' and 'Give the baby doll a kiss'. He also indicates that he understands questions like 'Do you want your bottle?' In fact, there's no real way to measure how much a baby does understand, but it easily surpasses his ability to say words.

12 to About 18 Months

Comprehension continues to outpace production. It's estimated that a child comprehends about fifty different words by 12 months of age; yet he usually doesn't say that many until 18 or 20 months.

A toddler of this age points to familiar people, animals and objects when requested. He shows his own shoe or even a doll's shoe. He throws a ball when asked. In fact, he has many ways to demonstrate how much he understands.

After a child says his first words, his spoken vocabulary tends to grow one word at a time. Word rates vary, but most children have a vocabulary of thirty to fifty words by 18 months. He definitely delights in this new skill. He demands objects by pointing and vocalizing single words. He often names things and people just for the sheer pleasure of pronouncing the words and attaching them to the appropriate objects. When someone talks to him, he might echo prominent words or the last word in the sentence. He usually mispronounces words, because he lacks the muscular structure to formulate difficult word sounds, but even so most words are understandable to family members.

18 to 36 Months

During this period a toddler's vocabulary grows very rapidly. In one large study in the United States, the 24-month-olds had an average speaking vocabulary of 200 words. But that was the *average*; the range was from 30 to over 400 words, giving more evidence that each child develops at his own pace. By 3 years, a child has a speaking vocabulary of several hundred words. Not surprisingly, these words are the most common and important ones. Even though the English language has over 400,000 words, only about 500 words are used most often; in fact, they make up about 90 per cent of typical adult conversations. A 2-year-old has mastered nearly half of these 500 words, and the 3-year-old almost all of them.

The other major development during this age span is putting words together to form sentences. Before this age, a child usually speaks in one-word utterances. At some stage after about 18 or 24 months, he combines them, which greatly increases his ability to express himself. For instance, up to this point he might have said 'more' or 'juice' to let you know he wanted another drink. But since he spoke only one word, you couldn't be absolutely sure what he intended. What does he want more of? Or, what is he trying to say about juice? Now that he can say 'More juice' there's no questioning his intention! These phrases almost always reflect correct syntax, with proper subject–verb or verb–object order. For example, a toddler probably would not say 'Juice more'.

After 24 months a child begins using longer and longer phrases so that by 30 months he really talks in sentences of three or more words.

COMMON QUESTIONS

Naturally, language growth doesn't proceed without hidden mysteries or apparent mistakes. Here are some of the topics that concern many parents I know.

How Do First Words Appear?

First words apparently grow out of babbling, although no one can state exactly how. Babbling is a universal language; babies around the word babble the same rich assortment of sounds, from the softer slurs of the Romance languages to the clicking sounds of some African dialects. It seems that babies continue to use the word sounds that are reinforced in their own language, and discard the others.

The process of turning babbles into words appears to involve three conditions:

1. A baby's physical ability to make particular sounds.
2. A baby's inborn interest in imitating words and word sounds he hears frequently.
3. Parents' encouragement to repeat sounds and turn them into words.

For an example, let's look at the word *dada*. It's a common first word, probably because:

1. The *da* sound is easy for a baby to make.
2. Parents often talk about a father, usually calling him Daddy.
3. Whenever a baby says *dada* even by accident, ecstatic parents usually encourage repeats: 'He said "dada"! He knows me! Say "dada" again.' When the baby, delighted with this new power, complies, parents again react enthusiastically, so he tries again. In time, with parents' encouragement and gentle correction, *dada* becomes *Daddy*. Other common words, like *Mama*, *baybee*, *car* and *doggie* probably evolve in much the same way.

Why These Particular Words?

Even though every toddler hears and comprehends hundreds if not thousands of words, most toddlers have a very similar early speaking vocabulary. It's obvious why words like *Mummy* and *Daddy* appear in almost every early vocabulary. It's also obvious that most early words are things a toddler can pronounce or at least approximate easily. But that could be the case for thousands of things. Why is there surprising uniformity between the speaking vocabularies of different young children in the same culture?

Language specialist Katherine Nelson has studied early vocabularies, looking in particular at the first fifty different words that children in her study spoke. Over 65 per cent of those first words are nouns: the names or labels of things the toddlers find important. Words that most toddlers use include *ball*, *car*, *doggie*, *Mummy*, *Daddy*, *juice*. The remaining types of spoken words are action words (*look*, *bye-bye*, *give*), modifiers (*mine*, *big*), and personal–social words (*please*, *no*). When the nouns are examined more closely, other interesting patterns emerge. Why do so many toddlers use such words as *ball*, *car* and *shoes*, yet rarely say the names of objects surely just as familiar and easy to pronounce: *tree*, *coat*, *shirt*?

The conclusion: toddlers first use the names of objects that they can act on, or that move in interesting ways. A *ball* is active and you can do so many things with it; a *tree* is just 'there'. A *car* zooms along and makes sounds and you can ride in it. *Shoes* are something a toddler can at least take off if not put on. But a *coat* and *shirt* are beyond his abilities to manage himself; these are things he can't act on all that well. Even favourite food words tend to be *juice* and *bikky* or *bikit* (for biscuit), because these are things the toddler can feed to himself. The toddler knows what a tree and coat and shirt and hundreds of other nouns are; it's just that, spontaneously, he's far less likely to include them in his early vocabulary of spoken words.

For fun, keep a list of your own toddler's growing vocabulary, and see how closely his first words match the types of words that were found to be so popular in this study.

Is Bad Pronunciation a Problem?

For toddlers, mispronunciation is the standard, not the exception. Most speech sounds, especially those involving complex co-ordination of the tongue, lips and larynx, are difficult to make. Sounds like *sh*, *spa*, *spra*, *ch* and *th*, for instance, are frequently mispronounced even by almost half of all 3-year-olds. Your toddler constantly substitutes a simpler sound for one more difficult: *dat* for *that*, *pitty* for *pretty*, *care* for *chair*, and the like.

Why Do Toddlers Mix Up Words?

A toddler often uses a single word to refer to several different objects. He might call every man *Daddy*; or call every round object *ball*, be it a stone, the moon, a radish, an orange; or everything with four legs – pony, horse, pig or cow – a *doggie.* In other words, he refers to a variety of objects, actions, or people by the same name if they have one or more features in common.

Scientists call this *over-extension.* When your toddler uses the same word for two objects, it can mean:

o He truly doesn't recognize the difference between two things; if he has never seen an orange before, he might really believe an orange *is* a ball.

o He doesn't know the name of one of them. If he's new to pigs, it's logical to believe that a pig is a type of dog.

o He doesn't know how to say the name of one object. He clearly knows that every man is not his daddy. Yet if he doesn't know the word *man*, he naturally substitutes the closest word he does know.

Your toddler loves to talk and to name things. Yet because his vocabulary lags behind his comprehension, he often lacks the correct word. So he does the best with what he knows. He over-extends less as he learns new vocabulary words, and as he truly does learn the differences between seemingly similar objects.

——— GENERAL WAYS TO HELP ———

Talk to your baby! Even from the earliest months, even when you two aren't actively playing together, talk to your baby. He needs to hear the words and sounds of language in order to produce them himself. Talking also helps to keep him in touch with you, from across the room or wherever you happen to be. It lets him know how special he is. When you're cooking dinner, tell him why you add certain spices to that pasta sauce, or why you knead the pastry dough. If you're tidying up, tell him why you put the cups in that cupboard, the silverware in its special drawer. Or if you just need someone to spill your heart to, turn to your baby. You can be sure he won't gossip behind your back.

Bear in mind that this does not suggest you turn into a chattering magpie. Too much talk, like almost anything in excess, is boring and dilutes its effect. But it does mean that talking to your baby is valuable – whatever his age.

When you and your young child play together, talk about his toys. Describe them in as many ways as you can, repeating important words frequently and using plenty of adjectives. 'See your ball, Joshua, your big, yellow ball? Look – it bounces. I'm going to roll the ball – can you catch it?' Encourage him to 'talk' by asking questions and pausing for him to respond, even if only with a wave or a wiggle at early ages. Later he'll supply words; later still enter into more realistic conversations.

Be sure to name objects for him – things he's looking at as well as toys you're playing with together. He loves learning names of things well before he can say them himself. Name body parts at bath and changing time. As you undress him, a cheerful 'Let's take off your shirt – lift up your arms' is much more educational and pleasant than undressing him in silence. Talk about the groceries as you shop, and again when you unpack them at home. Take a tour of your house, stopping frequently to talk about all the things you and he see.

Always remember: talking should be light, easy, natural and fun. If you start sounding too much like a language teacher, it loses spon-taneity, and enjoyment dwindles for both of you.

Also remember that it's probably best not to pressure your toddler too much as he's trying his new language skills. Admonishments to 'Say *doggie* for your grandma, come on, say *doggie* for Grandma', when he's not in the mood, or insisting that he repeat a word until he pronounces it correctly, may discourage his attempts to talk. On the other hand, ecstatic enthusiasm at his *every* attempt to say a word is out of place, too. Over-abundant praise for an action not worthy of such accolades can overwhelm your toddler.

Draw your child's attention to new areas of interest.

Some Specifics

○ When your young baby makes sounds, lean your face close to his and make the same sound back. He'll probably smile – and may even make the sound again for your response.

○ When he begins to babble, babble back and encourage him to babble back to you. See how long you can keep the string of babbles going.

○ Once your baby begins saying words, encourage him to repeat the names of objects after you say them: 'A nice red cup, filled with juice. Here's your cup, Benjamin. Can you say *cup*?' At first he'll probably just say part of the word, like *ca*, or might mispronounce it as *dup*. That's fine – it's a good start. Encourage these attempts by modifying and expanding: 'That's right, it's a *cup*. A red cup full of juice.'

○ Gentle correction and expansion are the best ways to encourage your toddler as well. If he calls out 'goggie' when your household canine races across the garden, you can respond with, 'That's right, that's a doggie. Doesn't he run fast!' Or when he states 'Daddy go' after his father leaves the house, you might say, 'Yes, Daddy has gone to the shops. What do you think he might buy?' This concluding question invites your toddler to continue the conversation if he likes.

○ You might need to act as occasional interpreter when your toddler talks to other people. Some of his pet words and idiosyncratic pronunciations will be incomprehensible to outsiders. Always let him try first, but step in when it's obvious that communication is failing.

○ At some point your toddler starts asking questions: 'What dat?', 'Who dat?' Sometimes it's questions, questions all day long. Most of these are legitimate requests for information, marking his fascination with learning names. However, sometimes these questions probably are merely a means of getting attention, as many parents have always suspected. Try to be patient, and answer him as best you can. But if you're busy with other things, or are just too tired to respond to his enquiries, it's quite acceptable to tell him that you need a break.

—————— PICTURES AND BOOKS ——————

Books are the traditional way to enhance your baby's language skills. Hearing you read aloud helps him learn about the rhythms of language, grammar and sentence structure, and the sounds of words. Books build his vocabulary; they bring to him pictures of objects that he rarely encounters in his everyday life, such as baby animals. Reading together is a lovely emotional experience for you both, too.

I've found that babies usually go through typical stages in their interest in books:

○ Up to about 5 or so months, a baby usually likes looking quietly at pictures while listening to his parent talk about them. He rarely tries to handle the book.

○ From 5 to about 9 months, a baby usually tries to handle a book as he does most objects: mouthing, pulling, twisting, and so forth. When he does concentrate on the book as a book, he might pat the pages and babble along as you talk about the pictures.

○ After 9 months, a baby shows increasing interest in books for their intended purpose. He looks at, pats, and points to pictures, tries to turn the pages (often a few at a time if they're made of paper), and also attempts to say words.

○ During toddlerhood he shows increasing interest in books, first concentrating on the pictures. When he is nearly 2 years old, he enjoys plot and storyline as well.

Pictures for Beginning Readers

For the first year or more you don't really read picture books to your baby. You talk about the pictures in ways you invent. So the first books can be pictures of any appropriate type, both in traditional books with pages or in less conventional formats. For instance, the Eye Targets (page 18) and Picture Parade (page 21) are both unconventional books. So are the following two homemade toys.

The room-decorating Picture Line (page 126) is a picture 'book' that's spread horizontally across the nursery wall. The clothespeg-holder system lets you easily change the display whenever you come across a new picture your baby would like. To play, hold your baby close so he can see each picture as you talk about it.

Five- to nine-month-olds handle books like they do toys – roughly – so board or vinyl ones are best.

Boxed Pictures is a three-dimensional 'book' that's perfect for the baby who loves handling his reading materials; he can't rip the pages because there aren't any. To read: talk about the pictures one by one, as you would with pictures in a book. To play: your baby can drum on this cube with his hands, tumble it over like a ball, and (if you make several) build things with these colourful light blocks when he's older.

PICTURE LINE

Ideal Intro Age: 3 months
Age Range: 3 to 12 months

Tools and Materials

☆ Long piece of clothesline

☆ 2 hooks

☆ Several pinch-type clothespegs

☆ Magazines or other sources of pictures

Instructions

1. Thread clothespegs on to the clothesline.
2. Tie a loop in each end of the clothesline and hang it up on hooks screwed into the wall. The line itself should be about level with your head.
3. From the clothespegs, hang pictures that your baby might like. Choose those showing bright colours, familiar objects, animals and faces. You can find lots of appropriate pictures in magazines. Or you can use pictures from a calendar, choose an appealing poster, or buy reproductions of famous paintings at your local art gallery. Maybe this will help your baby develop a lifelong interest in fine art.

HINT: When your baby becomes a toddler, turn this clothesline into the On-the-Wall Scrapbook (page 168).

This homemade Picture Line turns the nursery wall into a picture 'book'.

BOXED PICTURES

Ideal Intro Age: 6 months
Age Range: 6 to 18 months
(see page 128)

Tools and Materials

☆ Plain gift box with lid; use the square, cube type – about 15 cm (6 in) or larger – not the long, flat type

☆ Magazines or other sources of pictures

☆ Scissors

☆ All-purpose household glue (non-toxic)

Instructions

1. Glue the lid on to the box.
2. Cut appropriate pictures out of magazines. Remember: babies like faces, animals and familiar objects (bottles, cups, pieces of clothing, toys, flowers). Glue a picture on each face of the box. Make sure you glue completely around the very edge of each picture so that your baby can't pick it off.

Homemade Boxed Pictures are great for physical
readers, since there are no pages to rip.

Using Books

These suggestions apply mostly to picture books for babies and toddlers. The text, if any, in these books is minimal and merely a
springboard to get you going. Older toddlers also like storybooks with
a plot and text that you read word for word. Even so, you can continue
to talk about the pictures as well:

○ Point to and even tap on a pictured object as you talk about it. Trace
   your finger around its outline. Repeat its name in a variety of sen-

Encourage your toddler to point to pictured objects as
you talk about them.

tences. Describe it completely, using lots of adjectives. Make up a
little story about it. Ask lots of questions, too – these involve your
child. Invite him to trace or pat the object. When he's old enough to
imitate sounds, ask him to join in vocally. For example:

'Well, look, Paul, here's a puppy, a baby puppy. See the puppy?
(*Trace*) She's such a funny puppy, a funny brown puppy. Look, she's
wagging her long tail (*point*). Let's call her Barker, just like Aunt
Helen's puppy. Look at Barker's fuzzy brown ears – oh, look (*point*),

her ears are pink inside. Do you see her ears? Can you show me the puppy's ears? That's right – fuzzy brown ears. And look at her tongue – a red tongue. Barker has a red tongue. (*Point*) I think this puppy is going to lick the little boy (*point*) with her tongue. Yes, she is. Barker is going to give the boy a kiss, a wet lickety kiss. Do you want a kiss, a puppy kiss? (*Comply*) Can you give me a puppy kiss, too? (*He does*) How nice. A nice wet puppy kiss. What does a puppy say? She says, "Ruffff, ruffff." Barker says, "Ruffff, ruffff." Can you sound like Barker? Can you sound like a puppy? Good!'

Then, if your baby is still interested in the puppy picture, talk about some other elements, or make up a brief tale about what the puppy might do next.

○   Sometimes your toddler points to an object unprompted. Follow his cues and expand: 'Oh, yes, there's the baby bear, and all his friends are leaving. Is he waving bye-bye? I think he is. Can you wave bye-bye? Say "bye-bye" to friendly baby bear.'

○   When looking at picture books of animals, make their funny noises. Ask your toddler to imitate you. When he knows his animal sounds by heart you can skip the demonstration. Point to any beast and ask, 'What does the —— say?' You can also make the sounds of vehicles and invite imitation.

○   If the book has a recurring character, ask your toddler to find it on every page: 'Can you find the gold bug in this picture?'

○   Always look to your child for cues. Is he getting bored? Go to the next picture. Does he want to linger? Pause as long as he likes. Is he restless, does he strain against you? Maybe book time is over. Does your toddler bring you a book? It's time to start again.

Sometimes this, too, happens: your toddler brings you a favourite book, begging your attention. Fine. You put aside your cup of coffee and newspaper, get all cosy on the sofa, open to page one, and then . . . shift, squirm, wiggle, he's struggling to get down and do something else. Fine. Seven minutes later, he's back with another book and that heart-melting look on his face. You put down the chequebook and pen and move to the sofa. This session lasts for three pages before the fidgeting sets in. He's off again. Then five minutes later. . . . Accede as long as your patience holds out, then promise that you'll read later as you're too busy now. And keep your promise.

o   And the most important suggestion of all – have fun! Be dramatic, and use different voices for different characters. Sing little songs or make up chants. Add sound effects – 'Here's the little yellow taxi, "s-c-r-e-e-e-e-c-c-h-h", he goes round the corner, "Beep beep," he calls, "Get out of my way."' Your ebullience and infectious enjoyment bring a book to life.

In addition to the books you and your young child share together, he'll sometimes just like hearing you read aloud whatever *you* like to read – the newspaper, a magazine article, a novel or short story. The content doesn't matter to him; the warmth and security of your voice do. Reading aloud can even calm a restless baby; and lying snugly, just listening to a bedtime story, certainly is a lovely way to drift into sleep.

Choosing Books for Babies and Young Toddlers

Each year hundreds of new baby–toddler books are published, so you can expect an eye-popping array when you visit the bookshop or library. What are the favourite titles? Who knows! We once surveyed sixteen mothers and four teachers of babies from 2 to 12 months old, asking each to list the five books she and her baby (or her 'pupils') liked most. The combined results included over seventy different titles! Much more interesting, though, are the features listed below which the favourite books share. They might help you to choose the best books for *your* baby.

CONTENTS

o   Clear, colourful, realistic pictures with uncluttered backgrounds.

o   Action-orientated pictures rather than merely static objects to name.

o   Pictures showing things that babies themselves typically do: eating, sleeping, playing with toys, having a bath, playing peekaboo and other familiar games.

o   Pictures showing clear and varied facial expressions, so that parents can talk about feelings and emotions.

o   Pictures showing familiar objects, especially in use.

○ Pictures of objects or activities that inspire sounds: animals (especially baby animals), vehicles, babies clapping their hands, and the like.

○ Brief text or storyline, if any. However, rhymes, poems, chants and songs are all popular.

PHYSICAL FEATURES

○ Durability! Especially for books the baby and toddler handle. Cardboard books are the favourites, thick vinyl books second. Cloth books are *not* recommended; after they're washed they become as limp as dishcloths.

○ Smooth, rounded corners, especially on cardboard books.

○ Washability. Favourite books get dirty.

○ Textures and other things to touch and handle.

Here are some suggestions:

> *Say Goodnight*; *Tickle, Tickle*; *Clap Hands* by Helen Oxenbury. *Baby's Day*; *Baby's Afternoon*; *Baby's Evening* by Penny Metcalfe. *The Baby's Catalogue* by Janet and Allan Ahlberg. *The Very Hungry Caterpillar* by Eric Carle. 'Playbooks' series – including *Bath Time*; *Busy Day*; *In the Park*; *Playtime* – by Chris Fairclough. *Where's Spot?* by Eric Hill.

Choosing Books for Older Toddlers

Older toddlers like pictures, too. They also like stories with a plot – beginning, middle and end. Again, there are hundreds of new titles yearly from which to choose, as well as the classics like *Peter Rabbit* and *Good Night, Moon* that have been around for decades. In another survey, we asked parents to tell us what types of toddler books were most successful in their homes, and what were the features or themes that made these books so successful. The most popular books shared one or more of the following themes. You might bear these in mind as you evaluate books for your own toddler:

○ The story is simple and repetitive; this makes it easy for a toddler to follow.

Some suggestions:

> *Percy to the Rescue*; *Thomas Goes to Town* by Rev. W. Awdry. *Bill and*

Stanley by Helen Oxenbury. *The Ugly Duckling* by Susan Hellard. *The Elephant and the Bad Baby* by Elfrida Vipont. *Dear Zoo* by Rod Campbell. *The Troublesome Pig* by Priscilla Lamont. *B is for Bear* by Dick Bruna. *Meg and Mog* by Helen Nicholl and Jan Pienkowski.

○ The text is full of rhythms and rhymes, including both poetry and silly rhyming words. *Mother Goose* and A. A. Milne's *When We Were Very Young* fall into this category.

Some other suggestions are:

Pop Goes the Weasel by Robert Crowther. *This Little Puffin* by Elizabeth Matterson. *Nicola Bayley's Book of Nursery Rhymes. Appley Dapply's Nursery Rhymes* by Beatrix Potter. *The Grand Old Duke of York* by Bernard Lodge. *Round and Round the Garden* by Sarah Williams.

○ The story and pictures invite parent and child to play with sounds. Stories about trains and other vehicles offer these opportunities. So do stories which contain nonsense words that sound funny.

Some suggestions:

Rosie's Walk by Pat Hutchins. *Mig the Pig* by Colin and Jacqui Hawkins. *Is Anyone Home?* by Ron Maris.

○ The main character has characteristics, feelings, emotions and behaviour that the toddler can easily identify with and understand. Good examples include the Paddington and Peter Rabbit books.

Some other suggestions are:

Benjamin Bear's Busy Days by Stefan Lemke. *The Story of Ferdinand* by Munro Leaf. *Where the Wild Things Are* by Maurice Sendak. *Mr Gumpy's Outing* by John Burningham. *Phoebe and the Hot Water Bottles* by Linda Dawson and Terry Furchgott. *The Little Train* by Graham Greene and Edward Ardizzone. *The Very Bad Bunny* by Marilyn Sadler. *Alpaca* by Rosemary Billam.

○ The storyline presents situations and routines the toddler himself often experiences; again, this helps him identify with the main character. Stories about going to bed, going off to playgroup, meeting new friends, and the like, fit here.

Some suggestions:

> *My Teddy; Naughty Teddy*; and others in the series by Juliet Brown and Helen Pask. 'Step-by-Step' series – including *Day Time; Night Time; Shopping; My House* – by Diane Wilmer. *Alex and the Baby; Alex's Bed* by Mary Dickinson. *My Naughty Little Sister and Bad Harry's Rabbit* by Dorothy Edwards. *I Want My Potty* by Tony Ross. *Doing the Washing* by Sarah Garland. *Dogger* by Shirley Hughes. *Sunshine* by Jan Ormerod. *Bunny Bakes a Cake* by Eve Rice.

o The story has social–emotional lessons. For example, it presents strong family relationships, or has a powerful moral lesson, or shows a weak character overcoming adversity.

Some suggestions:

> *Just Awful* by Alma Marshall Whitney. *Burglar Bill* by Janet and Allan Ahlberg. *Topsy and Tim* by Jean and Gareth Anderson. *Dear Daddy* by Philippe Dupasquier. *Emmie and the Purple Paint* by Dorothy Edwards. *Wilfrid Gordon Macdonald Partridge* by Mem Fox. *Angry Arthur* by Hiawyn Oram and Satoshi Kitamura. *Naughty Nigel* by Tony Ross. *Emma's Baby Brother* by Gunilla Wolde. *Grandmother's Tales* by Celia Berridge.

For other suggestions, ask the children's librarian at your local public library, or the proprietor of a good children's book shop.

Making Books

Homemade books are special because they can be tailored to your toddler's specific interest. They're easy to make, too, since a book is nothing more than picture-covered pages bound along one margin. Make lots.

The following suggested books are made with paper pages, so they're best for shared reading, and for the toddler who can either turn pages himself or is content to let you do it. You might want to use homemade books with your baby, too. After all, they're cheap. But always supervise, because a baby might rip up pages and chew – or choke – on the paper.

You can buy the basic supplies – report covers and punched paper – at any office supply shop or stationer.

GREAT BOOKS!

Ideal Intro Age: 12 months
Age Range: 12 to 36 months

Tools and Materials

For each book:

☆ Heavy paper report cover, with fasteners that accept 3-hole-punched paper

☆ Several sheets of 3-hole-punched paper

☆ Magazines and other sources of pictures

☆ Scissors

☆ Clear adhesive tape

Instructions

Fill the report cover with paper to make a blank book, then fill the pages with pictures you tape on. Suggested themes:

○ Christmas or Birthday Book: cover the pages with old greetings cards. These usually have bright colours, glitter, embossed fronts, cut-outs, and other sight-and-touch things toddlers love. Plus, each is a 'mini-book' your toddler can open and close before going on to the next.

○ Holiday Book: fill with postcards you've picked up on holiday, and with photographs you've taken. If your toddler went with you, this book will be a nice reminder that lets him relive the experience. If he didn't, it is a consolation that helps him feel involved, at least vicariously.

○ Supermarket Book: a book of labels from packages of favourite foods. Cut them from magazine advertisements or from the pack itself. When you and your toddler go shopping, let him find the real packs on the shelves.

○ All About Me: a book with pictures of your toddler's favourite things; and, of course, of your toddler himself! Let him help to choose the pictures to be included.

SURPRISE PICTURE BOARD

Ideal Intro Age: 18 months
Age Range: 18 to 36 months

Tools and Materials

☆ Letter-sized file folder

☆ Several sheets of blank
paper, 210×297 mm
($8\frac{1}{4} \times 11\frac{3}{4}$ in)

☆ Magazines and other
sources of pictures

☆ Ruler

☆ Stanley knife or hobby
knife

☆ Scissors

☆ Clear adhesive tape

Instructions

1. Open the file folder flat. Use the ruler and Stanley knife to cut four windows on the cover, as illustrated. Cut only three sides; the uncut side becomes the hinge.
2. Bend back each flap to make the hinge. Reinforce the hinges with tape, on both the facing and the reverse sides.
3. On each sheet of paper, tape four pictures in places that correspond with the windows. These can be photographs, postcards, pictures cut from magazines and catalogues or off toy boxes, things you draw, whatever.
4. To play, shut the file folder and slide a picture sheet inside. Your toddler opens a flap – and guesses the object or person.

———— MORE LANGUAGE PLAY ————

○ Not all stories are in books. Make up your own, some with your toddler as the thinly disguised hero. You can borrow plots from familiar fairy tales.

○ Not all pictures are in books. Give your toddler a small box filled with pictures – old photographs, postcards, giveaways and other advertising material that comes through the post. He'll love tipping them out, sorting through them, and putting them away. Play with him when you can, and talk about each picture.

○ Toddlers love lifting flaps in books to see what's behind them. They also love guessing the name when you point to an object and ask, 'What's that?' Combine these two interests into one Surprise Picture Board. You slip a sheet of pictures inside the folder; your toddler opens the flaps one by one as you ask him, 'What's that?'

———————— TO SUM UP ————————

Language has been called the most powerful, most versatile resource of civilization. Little wonder that a baby is born with a predisposition for learning it. And little wonder that parents value its development so highly. By creating a rich verbal environment for your child, through the ways suggested here and countless others of your own invention, you're helping him acquire one of his most valuable assets.

Water and 6 sand play

'No, no, keep your fingers out of the pudding!'

'Mustn't play with that — it's dirty!'

Sound familiar? Probably, because most young children relish messy play, partly because they truly *are* messy — they lack skilled co-ordination and self-restraint — and partly because it's so much fun just to explore squishy, sloppy, ever-changing materials.

One beauty of water and sand (and mud and dirt) play is that these materials are so unstructured. There's no right way to use them, nor any wrong way except maybe throwing or eating them. With them your child can explore freely. The resulting mess is not only unpunished, it's expected. And because the play is so free-form, water and sand are a nice counterbalance to the more structured toys your young child also enjoys. There are plenty more benefits, too, and lots of ways to expand water and sand play.

PLAYING WITH WATER

A baby plays with water almost from the first time she has a bath. She waves her arm — and something moves and plops lightly against her skin. Later she kicks — more movement, more sensations. These early explorations give way to the scooping, pouring, and scientific experimentation that mark true water play.

Most babies enjoy true water play once they can sit securely in the bath, usually at around 7 to 8 months if you use a plastic baby bath. The family bath is usually too slippery unless there is a rubber mat on the bottom. Once a baby is over this hurdle, water play becomes a joyful activity. It has enormous benefits as well. While playing with water, your young child:

○ Practises all kinds of arm–hand–finger skills and eye–hand co-ordination – splashing, filling, scooping, pouring, catching a bobbing object or a pouring stream.

○ Learns scores of new words when you participate – *empty, full, wet, dry, float, sink, cold, warm.*

○ Discovers early scientific principles, such as flotation and water power. ('What happens when I pour water over this paddle wheel?')

Water inspires fantasy play. For example, your toddler will probably bath a baby doll (just as she herself is bathed) or wash up the play dishes after a tea party. Your suggestions and encouragement expand the possibilities. You could invite your toddler to pretend she's a mermaid, a fish, a tugboat, the Loch Ness Monster, or any sea creature from one of her favourite books.

How else can you help? Set up play opportunities, supervise to make sure everything's going safely, provide interesting props, offer verbal encouragement and new words for her to learn, and (of course) join in when you can.

SAFETY NOTES

1. *Never* let your child play in or around water without your vigilant supervision. There's always a chance of drowning.
2. *Always* drain a paddling pool or other container after playtime. Any body of standing water is a drowning hazard.
3. *Never* let your child play in the bathroom unless you're there. She could drown in the toilet bowl.

Outdoor Play

o A traditional paddling pool is very popular for outdoor water play. The moulded plastic type is more durable than the inflatable-ring type.

o For more confined spaces, or times you don't want to use the paddling pool, fill a large bowl with water. Your child sits outside it to play – or even inside if the bowl accommodates both her and some favourite water toys. A large plastic washing up bowl or the old plastic baby bath is a good container.

o Let your toddler play with a hose, or frisk around under a sprinkler. Special idea: train a sprinkler so it sprays your toddler when she's in her paddling pool. Fantasy rain!

Indoor Play

o The bath is a natural playground. Store favourite bath toys in a drawstring mesh bag, and hang it on the shower head or taps between playtimes so the toys drip dry. Or store toys in a plastic bucket on the bathroom floor, and drain it frequently.

o Bath play needn't be limited to bathtime. Let your toddler play in the water-filled bath whenever you need to be in the bathroom for a while; for example, when you give it a thorough cleaning, or mend a leaky tap, or put your make-up on.

o Another idea: your toddler can sit in an empty bath and play with water that's in a bucket. She stays fairly dry, and so does the bathroom.

o If you can trust your older toddler to be careful, let her play with a container of water on a low table in the kitchen. Extra fun: add a squirt of washing up liquid to the water, and give your toddler a wire whisk so she can beat the water into a sudsy froth.

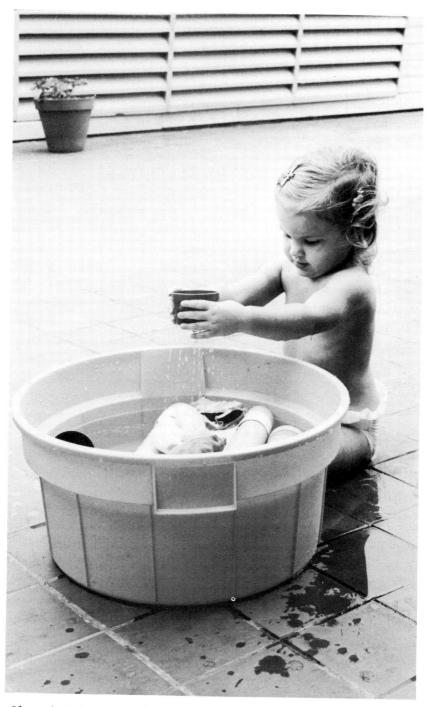

If you don't have space for a paddling pool, fill a large bowl with water;
your toddler sits outside it to play.

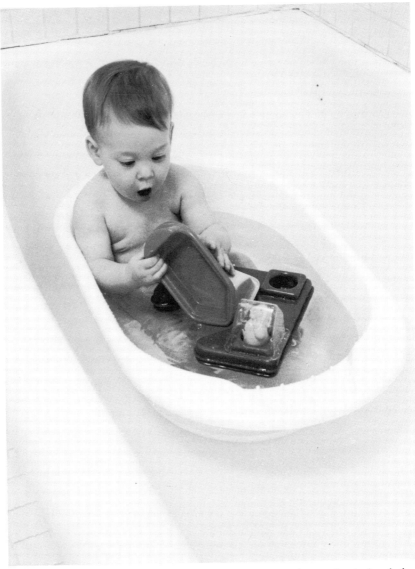

The baby bath, set into the ordinary bath, can help the newly sitting baby feel more confident for water play.

Good Water Toys

Plastic kitchen items such as cups with handles, sieves and strainers, plastic sifter, and measuring cups.

Sponges.

Balls which will not get waterlogged.

- Length of plastic tubing, if your toddler knows the difference between blowing and sucking.

- *Clean* squirt bottles, small enough for your toddler to hold and squeeze.

- Commercial water toys; those that manipulate water in a variety of ways, and that have removable parts which can be stacked and fitted together, will get extra play.

INFLATABLE BATH BOAT

This toy is designed for general water play and for fantasy. The plastic tub is a good container for filling with water via small cups. The holes make it a giant sieve; your toddler will love lifting up this toy to see the water sprinkle out. It can give rides to dolls and other seafaring passengers in make-believe games, too.

Ideal Intro Age: 12 months

Age Range: 12 to 36 months

Tools and Materials

☆ Inflatable water ring

☆ Hammer and large nail

☆ Plastic tub (ice cream or margarine container) that fits snugly inside the ring

Instructions

1. Use the hammer and large nail to punch several holes in the bottom of the plastic tub.
2. Inflate the water ring and wedge the tub into the centre.

PLAYING WITH SAND

Sand is a rather magical material. Because it can be scooped and poured like water, it offers many of water's benefits: skill development, concept learning, new vocabulary words. But it has special qualities: it can be dribbled into interesting patterns; it's good for drawing in, digging in, and hiding toys in. Add water and it becomes like dough that holds its shape when pressed and formed. Or you can press biscuit cutters into it to make designs. Add more water and it becomes runny. Not really a solid, not really a liquid, it's somewhere in between.

Good Sand Toys

Most water toys (cups, sieves, etc.); serving spoon or small shovel for digging; drumstick-like rod for drawing; plastic biscuit cutters; and toy vehicles and characters for the older toddler.

SAFETY NOTES

1. Always supervise sandpit play. Your child might try to eat or throw the sand.
2. Neighbourhood animals (especially cats) have a habit of using a sandpit for a toilet. Keep your home sandpit covered with a plastic sheet weighted at the corners, or a sheet of plywood.

The homemade twin-pooled Sand and Sea Playground on page 146 takes care of the cover question nicely. One pool is turned into a sandpit, the other is used as a paddling pool/sandpit lid. Admittedly, this idea is *not* inexpensive. However, if you're planning to buy or build a sandpit anyway, this one is very easy. And the extra paddling pool/lid means it will get used a lot more. Remember, too, that a sandpit and paddling pool remain favourite toys throughout the early years.

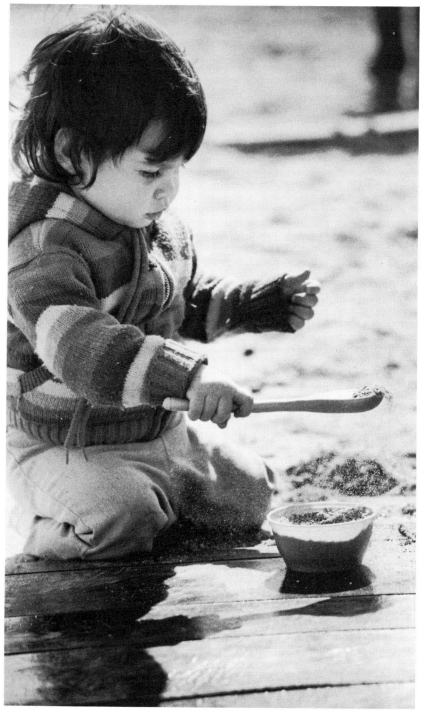

Sand is magical – not really solid, not really liquid.

SAND AND SEA PLAYGROUND

Ideal Intro Age: 9 months
Age Range: 9 to 36 months
FOR SUPERVISED PLAY ONLY

Tools and Materials

☆ 2 moulded plastic paddling pools, each with a rolled lip around the perimeter

☆ 3 wood planks, each about 1.25 m (4 ft) long, about 10 cm (4 in) wide, and at least 2.5 cm (1 in) thick

☆ Silver sand – plenty (from a builder's merchant)

☆ Electric drill and large bit – at least 6 mm ($\frac{1}{4}$ in)

☆ 2 large, strong, spring-type clamps or large 'G' clamps

Instructions

1. Decide where you want the sandpit to be located; once it's installed it will be hard to move. Some tips:

○ Ideally the spot should be partially shaded. If your baby likes to play in the sand for long periods, the sandpit (and she) can get very hot when totally exposed to the sun.

○ The ground should be level.

▶

2. Drill several water-drainage holes in the bottom of one pool (this will be the sandpit).

3. Set the sandpit on the three planks. These raise it slightly off the ground, so any water that gets inside can drain out.

4. Fill with sand, at least 10 cm (4 in) deep.

5. Use the other pool as a conventional paddling pool. It's best not to set it too near the sandpit, though, or your child will probably delight in pouring water from the pool into the sandpit.

6. When playtime's over, lay the paddling pool upside down on top of the sandpit, and clamp the two rims together. This lid keeps cats and rainwater out of the sand.

SAFETY NOTE: The clamps are NOT suitable toys; keep them away from your child.

One family turned a giant tractor tyre into a sandpit.

TO SUM UP

Water and sand, like the early art supplies discussed in Chapter 3, Activities for Hands (and Heads), are usually considered creative materials, since they give free rein to a child's imagination. The next chapter looks at another creative part of your young child's life – music.

sound 7
and music

Babies and toddlers are as fascinated by things that they hear as things they see and touch. Many child development experts label children as naturally musical. Babies can hear right from birth (actually, even in the womb), and enjoy listening to sounds and music from the first weeks. It's obvious they like hearing parents sing; traditionally, babies have been soothed to sleep with lullabies. Older babies coo and babble rhythmically without any encouragement. They bounce and sway to music and love to make sounds with toys. Toddlers march and dance spiritedly; join in songs that have a familiar, catchy verse; and make their own abstract music with an assortment of simple instruments. As Donna Brink Fox, a children's music expert at the Eastman School of Music in Buffalo, New York, recently pointed out: 'In fact, there seems to be no way to prevent children from displaying these musical behaviors, for during the preschool years music becomes both a means and an end, a fun way to help learn things, but also a purely expressive behavior important for its own sake.'

Like your baby's other abilities, there are several ways you can enjoy and enhance this inborn interest through play.

—— SETTING THE MUSICAL STAGE ——

Whether you want to sow the seeds of a musical career or to enlarge all your child's horizons, *your* interest in music probably affects his own.

Research shows that a child whose parents value music, who listen to music frequently and play musical games, generally has an increased enjoyment in and aptitude for music. This is similar to the situation regarding early readers – they tend to come from homes where parents read a lot both in general and with their child.

This general influence also has theoretical connections with true musical talent that may surface in later years. Music researcher Benjamin Bloom conducted a comprehensive study in the United States of talented young people, looking at many aspects of their backgrounds. His report concluded that 'Extremely talented people aren't born with extraordinary gifts. More likely, they become highly talented because of the way their parents raise them and the atmosphere in their homes.'

Your own interest in music is probably your child's greatest motivation.

EARLY BEGINNINGS

Hearing is the obvious foundation of music appreciation and development, and this sense is working even before birth. From about the fourth or fifth month of pregnancy, the unborn baby moves about more actively when his mother speaks loudly or makes a loud sound. Mothers-to-be have reported increased movement, too, when they type at an electric typewriter or have their teeth drilled by the dentist.

Some experts believe that a baby is influenced by such early experiences in the womb, and even recalls them after he's born. There's anecdotal evidence that pieces of music may become imprinted *in utero*. As American paediatrician T. Berry Brazelton related in a magazine article:

> A woman who is a pianist claims that she practiced a Chopin waltz over and over in the last month of her pregnancy. After the baby came she stopped playing, and it was not until he was 3 months old that she started again. One day she revived the Chopin waltz. Her baby had been kicking and gurgling in his playpen near the piano; when she began the waltz he stopped all activity, turned toward the piano and was transfixed. She is convinced that he remembered it. So am I.

In the delivery room a baby turns his head towards a sound and tries to discover where it is coming from. The newborn prefers human voices, and studies show that he can even distinguish his mother's voice from those of other people (more evidence of pre-natal stimulation!).

Babies not only hear, they can also distinguish between different sounds from a very early age. You probably see your baby react to various sounds in different ways. Sudden loud sounds and high-pitched tones (like a whistling kettle) may make him stiffen and cry. Calm, gentle sounds like a lullaby usually relax him. Experiments reveal that a baby's sound discrimination skills are even sharper than these everyday observable reactions. From about 8 weeks, babies in a research setting could tell the difference between two tones fairly close in pitch. Six-month-olds could perceive changes in melodies. All this laboratory and popular evidence suggests that babies are never too young to enjoy and in some way respond to sound and music.

General Play Tips

○ Let your baby listen to all the types of music you enjoy, from classical to rock, country to pop, jazz, musicals and opera, and everything in between. Sometimes music can be the focus of your experience – for instance, you and your baby might rock together in the rocking chair while listening to some relaxing piece. Or you might dance and sway together while listening to music with an upbeat tempo. Other times, music might serve more as accompaniment. As mentioned before in this book, rhythmic music can be used to enhance an exercise routine or some spirited jumping play.

Take your baby on a cultural tour of music you yourself might never have really listened to. Try ethnic music from other lands, religious music, tribal and folk songs, medieval chants and avant-garde composition. Many public libraries have a range of musical records and tapes that you can borrow.

Pay attention to your baby's response to the music you play. Some children are agitated by loud music, or music with uneven or unusual rhythms. Then again, every child has personal tastes, and your baby won't necessarily like everything that you might.

○ Consider putting a radio in the nursery. Quiet instrumental music might calm a restless baby and help him fall asleep on fretful nights.

○ Your older baby might enjoy sitting on the floor and swaying to music, especially when you do it, too. Try holding him in the standing position so that he can bounce and 'dance' along to the rhythm. Or pick him up and dance together. Waltz. Zip and twirl. When he can stand alone, hold his hands and dance like partners.

○ Your toddler loves to dance alone as well as with you. Just turn on the radio or stereo and let him devise his own choreography.

○ Remember those musical resources outside the home, like seaside or park bandstands, and parades. Most young children love marching music (as long as they are far enough away so that the music isn't too loud). You and your child might have a picnic while listening.

○ Don't forget that your singing adds terrifically personal music to your baby's world. You'll probably never have a more enraptured, appreciative audience.

○ Make a few songs part of the bedtime routine.

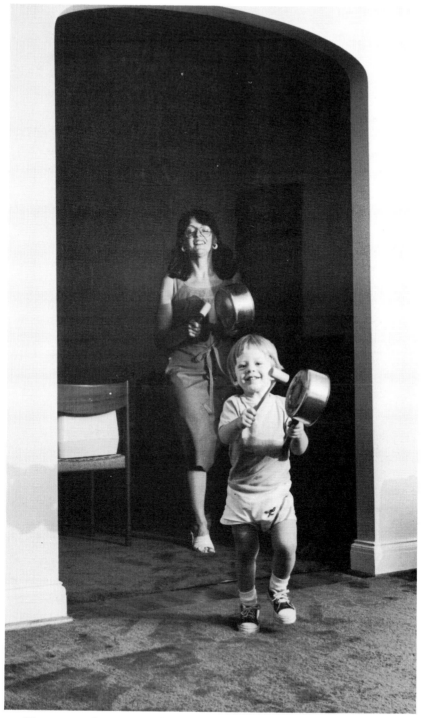

Have a parade – pans and wooden mallets make good instruments.

○ When your young child is getting fidgety in his carseat, launch into some favourite familiar tune, especially one that has lots of repetition, like 'Old MacDonald'. If you encourage him, he might join in, too – croon, babble, or sing a few words, depending on his skill level.

○ Playgroup leaders often bring chants and invented songs into many other activities. For example, they chant 'This is the way we wash our hands' (to the tune of 'Here We Go Round the Mulberry Bush') when cleaning toddlers' hands after arts play. Or they sing stories, or parts of stories, instead of speaking them. These can have very simple words and tunes – or even familiar tunes with new words inserted. They find that singing helps hold the baby's attention and enhances his developing vocabulary. Simple tunes can make it easier to learn and remember words. It's no secret that adults often recall advertising lyrics more easily and powerfully than merely spoken statements.

NURSERY RHYMES

Nursery rhymes combine singing (or chanting), movement, close contact with beloved parents, and elements of surprise. No wonder they've been cherished for centuries.

There are thousands of rhymes, enough to fill a book – or really, several books, because there are many nursery rhyme books available. I recommend you buy one. Until you have a chance, though, here are some favourite rhymes to get you started:

○ Make a fist. Chant this counting rhyme, exposing one finger at a time.

> Here is a beehive – where are the bees?
> Hidden away where nobody sees.
> Soon they come creeping out of the hive –
> One! Two! Three! Four! Five!

○ Pull your baby's fingers or toes in turn as you recite 'This Little Piggie'.

○ With your baby lying on his back, or sitting on your lap, facing you, pull his arms back and forth in a chug-a-chug motion while reciting 'Row, Row, Row Your Boat'.

○ Help your baby clap his hands as you sing 'Pat-a-cake, Pat-a-cake, Baker's Man'. Insert your baby's name in the last line: 'And put it in the oven for *Stephen* and me.' Poke him gently in the stomach when you

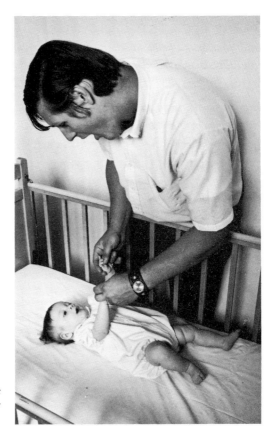

Pull your baby's arms in a chug-a-chug fashion to the words of 'Row, Row, Row Your Boat'.

reach his name. Soon he'll begin anticipating this tickly finale with mounting excitement.

○ 'Rock-a-bye Baby' is definitely among the top ten rhymes, if not the No. 1. Here's one way to enjoy it. Sit your baby on your lap, facing you, and hold him around the waist. While you sing the first three lines, rock him from side to side. When the bough breaks, of course, the cradle will fall. On the word *fall*, suddenly help your baby fall backwards slightly, then bring him back to sitting position. Once he has the hang of this version, let him fall further and further back. The variation adds to the surprise. You can also hold his hands rather than waist − but hang on tight when he falls!

○ Sit with your baby on the floor and chant 'Pop Goes the Weasel'. Again, sway him from side to side until the word *pop*; then lift him slightly off the floor.

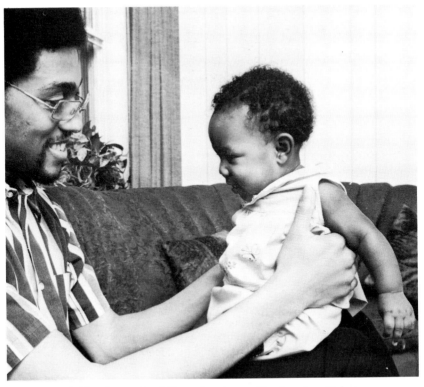

Add a dramatic 'fall' to the rhyme 'Rock-a-bye Baby'.

○ Bounce your baby on your knees (keep your toes on the floor and raise and lower your heels) while you chant a riding rhyme, such as:

> Ride a cock horse to Banbury Cross,
> To see a fair lady upon a white horse.
> With rings on her fingers and bells on her toes,
> She shall have music wherever she goes.

○ Your older baby or toddler also likes watching you perform little finger plays in time with an appropriate ditty. Favourites are 'Itsy Bitsy Spider' (or 'Eensy Weensy Spider') and 'Where Is Thumbkin?' A good simple finger-play songbook is worth buying, too.

FIRST INSTRUMENTS

Your baby's first musical instruments are all those soundmakers described in Chapter 3. Even before he is old enough to play with these himself, he likes hearing you make sounds with them.

BAND INSTRUMENTS

Ideal Intro Age: 15 months
Age Range: 15 to 36 months

Tools and Materials

☆ Various things, depending
on the instruments you
make (see below)

Instructions

1. Clappers: screw D-shaped drawer handles on to two blocks of wood, each about 15 cm (6 in) long, 7.6 cm (3 in) wide, and 2.5 cm (1 in) thick.
2. Rhythm Sticks: cut two pieces of wooden dowelling, each about 30 cm (12 in) long and 2.5 cm (1 in) in diameter; your toddler beats these together.
3. Shakers: fill a metal screw-top sugar shaker with some jar lids too large for your toddler to put into his mouth (in case he should open the shaker). Another favourite: *loud* baby rattle.
4. Cymbals: screw a wooden cabinet knob on the bottom of each of a pair of aluminium pie plates. Another favourite: two saucepan lids that don't have rims on the underside.
5. Drum: give your toddler a small saucepan and a wooden mallet beater.

HINT: Saucepans and lids and baking pans are wonderful instruments, but constant music play will dent and batter them. It makes sense to buy your toddler his own set at a charity or second-hand shop or jumble sale. If you like, store these and other instruments in a large cardboard box with appropriate decorations – musical notes, a drum, etc. – on the outside. Draw them with markers, or cut pictures from magazines and glue on.
SAFETY NOTE: Sand down the rough edges of all pieces of wood. Surfaces should be smooth to the touch and all corners should be rounded.

From about 6 or 7 months, your baby beats on a drum-like object with his hands or an appropriate drumstick.

○ Good drums: cooking pots or plastic mixing bowls turned upside down, small cardboard boxes, series of upside down aluminium baking pans.

○ Good drumsticks: cooking spoons (metal or wooden), small wooden mallet, hand-held rattles (they make a rattle sound and a clumping sound!). It's best to supervise play with any drumstick that has a small end your baby might put into his mouth.

Your toddler is ready for simple rhythm band instruments – maracas, cymbals, rhythm sticks, a xylophone, and the like. Have a parade – you, your toddler, and any other children and adults available can march around clanging and shaking and tooting and ringing. It may not sound like music to you, but from cacophony come modern symphonies.

CHILDREN'S RECORDS

Besides all the recorded music *you* like, your toddler enjoys some special children's records with simple songs and musical activities geared for his age group. These are also fun for you and him to listen to together; and they'll give you ideas of other musical games appropriate for toddlers. Look in the children's section of record shops.

TO SUM UP

Early music is many things: from your baby's first cry to rhythmic cooing and babbling to singing snatches of songs along with you; from tentatively shaking a rattle to marching about beating a drum; from listening to a lullaby to clapping his hands along with a 'Songs for Toddlers' record. Through the early play described here, you're helping to build his musical 'talent' and appreciation in a joyous context.

that's me! 8

The early years are a time of learning, and one topic that particularly interests your toddler is *herself*. Who am I? What do I look like? What am I made of? What makes me unique? This process of self-discovery, or self-recognition as it's sometimes called, begins when she's born and never really ends. We grow and change and discover ourselves throughout life.

As parents you are responsible for helping your child develop a strong and positive image of herself. One way you do this is by providing a solid sense of security, so that she views the world as a safe and secure place. This you give through care, support, nurturing, encouragement, praise, sympathy, understanding – in sum, through love and all it entails. These things a book can't teach.

Another, more fundamental way is by helping her learn about herself – what she looks like, the names and functions of parts of her body, an idea of her own unique being.

Your child is your companion on her self-discovery adventure. Everything she does helps her learn about herself – what she can and cannot do, what she likes and dislikes.

Throughout these early years she also exhibits different kinds of behaviour – sometimes endearing, sometimes baffling, sometimes even seemingly negative – that enhance and reflect her developing sense of self. Here are some highlights and ways you can help her learn 'That's me!'

WHAT AM I MADE OF?

Starting at about 1 or 2 months, your baby occasionally glances at her own outstretched hand as it passes through her line of vision. Most developmental psychologists believe that at this early age, she doesn't

A young baby isn't really sure whether her hand is part of her.

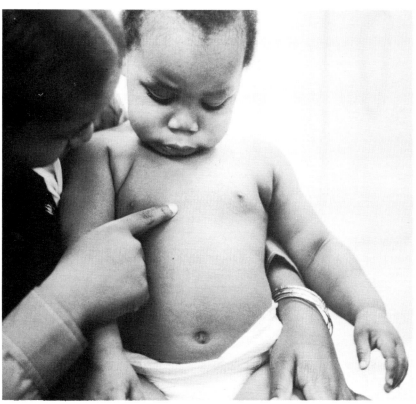

Naming games help your baby learn who she is and what she's made of.

realize it's a part of her any more or less than she thinks a toy is a part of her. But within a few months she stares at her hand more deliberately, and plays with her own hands and fingers. By now she has also experienced holding and releasing objects. It's believed that she can now distinguish between what is her and what isn't.

Starting at around 5 or 6 months, a baby explores not only her hands, but also her feet, hair, nose, ears, genitals – every part of her body within reach. This continues well into the toddler years as she seeks to learn what each part feels like and how it works.

The best way to help her learn about her body is the simple naming game that almost every parent instinctively plays. As you point to and name each part of her face and body, add a few words about its function. 'This is your nose, Jessica. We smell things with our nose.' Naming games are ideal for bathtime, changing time, almost any time you two play together.

WHAT'S MY NAME?

Your baby's name is a distinctive part of her individuality. Use it often when you speak to her. Near the end of her first year she links her name to herself, and points to herself correctly when asked, 'Where's [baby's name]?' Most children begin calling themselves by their name at around 2 years of age.

WHO'S IN THAT MIRROR?

A mirror helps your baby learn what she looks like, so make mirror games part of playtimes together:

○ Put a large, unbreakable mirror in your baby's cot. She's fascinated by her reflection because this 'picture' is always different. And it moves. Attach the mirror securely to the cotside so it doesn't topple over.

○ Let your 2- or 3-month-old look into a hand mirror. Talk about the different parts of her face. Starting at about 6 months or so, she might like to pat, talk to, and even kiss her new friend.

○ Hold your baby up so she can see herself in wall mirrors, too. Or help her sit on a dressing table so she can see herself in the mirror. Don't leave her alone, though.

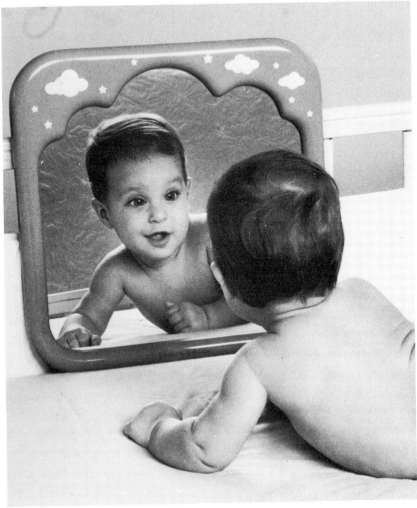

When does a baby recognize herself? Probably between 18 and 24 months.

o   Play some mirror peekaboo. Hold your baby on your lap and position a
    hand mirror where she can see her face. Tilt it so she disappears:
    'Where's Carla?' Tilt it back so she reappears: 'There's Carla! There she
    is! Peekaboo!'

o   From about 9 months on, hold your baby in your arms as you dance
    together in front of a full-length mirror. She enjoys watching as well as
    feeling the action.

o   Don't forget — that three-way mirror in a shop's fitting room is
    particularly fascinating. It creates three babies at once.

Does She Know Who It Is?

At what age does a baby looking in a mirror realize that she's seeing herself rather than 'another baby'? The answer isn't absolute, but here's some evidence.

One study by researcher Tiffany Brown placed 3-month-olds face to face with a mirror and with another baby the same age. On the whole, these babies looked for longer periods at the mirror but reacted more animatedly to the live babies. This suggests that a 3-month-old can tell the difference between a reflected image and a real baby, but it doesn't prove that the subjects knew they were looking at themselves.

In a study by psychologists Bennett Berthenthal and Kurt Fischer, each parent dressed her baby in a special vest that supported a hat about 15 cm (6 in) above the baby's head. (At this point, the baby did not realize the hat existed.) Then the baby was placed in front of a mirror, and the parent drew attention to the reflected hat and asked her baby to find it. The researchers reasoned that if a baby looked or reached up at the real hat, rather than trying to grab the reflected image, she must have known it was she — not another baby — in that mirror.

The babies in this study searched correctly at about 10 months on average. But again, did this mean the babies recognized themselves, or was it simply that they knew the difference between a real baby and a reflected one?

A simple and clever study was devised. Each mother–baby pair was brought into the laboratory where the mother secretly dabbed a spot of rouge on her baby's nose. Then the baby was placed in front of a mirror. If the baby pointed to or touched or otherwise examined the spot, the researchers reasoned, then she must realize she's looking at herself. Here's what the researchers found:

o Babies from 6 to about 14 months cooed and babbled and patted their reflections, but none examined the spot.

o About half of the 18- to 20-month-olds examined the spot, demonstrating that they recognized themselves.

o Nearly two-thirds of the 21- to 24-month-olds recognized themselves.

In another examination by Berthenthal and Fischer, each child looked into a mirror while her mother pointed to the reflection and asked, 'Who's that?' If the child stated her name or used an appropriate pronoun she was judged as recognizing herself. On average, this happened at 24 months.

So when does your child recognize herself in the mirror? Probably between 18 and 24 months. Another study found that children recognize themselves in photographs at about the same age, too.

'SECURITY BLANKETS'

Another way a child exhibits her growing sense of self is by adopting a 'security blanket'.

As discussed in Peekaboo (page 47), after 6 months a baby begins to realize that she is separate and distinct from her parents, and as she grows increasingly independent, she suffers bouts of insecurity. During these temporary travails she often turns for comfort to a dummy, her thumb, or a favourite 'security blanket' when you aren't available.

Cuddlies – a blanket, a stuffed animal, an old soft cloth – are quite common. A recent survey found that about 60 per cent of the 18-month-olds studied had a favourite cuddly. An almost identical proportion of 3-year-olds in the same study were still attached to cuddlies.

A cuddly is so popular because it serves, in the words of child development specialist D. W. Winnicott, as a 'transitional object'. This nice, familiar friend helps a child weather the transition from complete emotional dependence on her parents to partial independence. By relying on a cuddly, your child shows that she is developing her own mechanisms for dealing with stress and insecurity.

Another study found that a cuddly is just as effective as the mother's presence in helping a toddler adjust to unfamiliar situations. So if your child adopts one, be sure to carry it with you whenever she might face some situation that might trouble her, especially if you can't be with her every moment.

Bear in mind that not all children adopt a cuddly. As mentioned above, some rely on their thumb, a dummy, or activities like rhythmic rocking or fingering and twisting their hair to help get through temporary rough times.

The Huggable Butterfly, one of the simplest homemade stuffed toys I know, is a good candidate for becoming a favourite security blanket. It's bright and colourful, easy to grasp and hug, and the towelling texture is quite comforting.

A cuddly can help a young child cope with stressful times.

HUGGABLE BUTTERFLY

Ideal Intro Age: 6 months
Age Range: 6 to 36 months

Tools and Materials

☆ 2 hand towels, each no larger than 30×45 cm (12×18 in); choose ones with broad stripes or other bold patterns

☆ Piece of thick, soft wool, at least 60 cm (24 in) long

☆ Polyester fibrefill, shredded foam, or other machine-washable stuffing

☆ Sewing machine or needle and thread

Instructions

1. Place the towels together, with the patterned sides (if any) face to face, and sew around three sides.
2. Turn this pocket right-side-out, stuff tightly, and sew closed the remaining side to create a pillow.
3. Loop the wool two or three times around the centre of this pillow, pull *tight* to form two butterfly 'wings', and knot *securely* with a double or triple knot.
4. Trim off the excess wool, right down to the knot.

IS IT SELFISHNESS?

'Me!' 'Mine!' At some point these become your toddler's watchwords. Are they, as many parents fear, the sign of growing selfishness? Usually not. They're merely another way your toddler reveals her developing sense of self.

At some time during her second year, your toddler starts recognizing that some objects are *hers*, while others are *Daddy's* or *Mummy's* or *sister's*, and emphatically distinguishes between 'mine' and 'yours'.

Sometimes this sense of possession will prompt shouts of '*No!*' when another person, especially another child, tries to play with her toys.

Rather than piggishness, these outbursts reflect a toddler's insecure sense of personal identity. Since one way she defines herself is through her possessions – *my* shoes, *my* coat, *my* toys – she naturally feels a bit threatened when a part of herself is snatched away. In time, though, she'll develop a fuller, more mature understanding of herself, and will be more relaxed about sharing her worldly goods. This will be a sign that she's becoming more secure in her newfound identity.

But why does she have to be so possessive at first, you might ask. Well, think about other skills she's been developing – skills like walking or saying a first word. At every new milestone she tended to overdo it a bit. The same is true about the steps in discovering herself.

ALL ABOUT ME

Here are some more ways to help your toddler learn all about herself.

Family Photo Albums

Share with your toddler family albums filled with photos that chronicle her life: the pregnant mother; coming home from the hospital; first birthday; and all the other moments you've captured on film. Remind her that once she was a little baby, 'But you're such a big girl now!' Talk about other family members, too, using appropriate titles like grandmother and aunt and brother, so she understands a bit about her family as well.

Family photo albums help your child learn about herself and her connection to other family members.

ON-THE-WALL SCRAPBOOK

This novel room decoration spells out highlights of your toddler's past in an easy-to-follow sequential format. Hold her in your arms and go down the line, talking about each picture or object displayed. Naturally, she won't understand the significance of this for months, but it's a nice way to tell a living story. And gradually she will learn what it means.

Ideal Intro Age: 12 months

Age Range: 12 to 36 months

Tools and Materials

☆ Photographs and various favourite items

☆ Long piece of clothesline

☆ Several pinch-type clothespegs

☆ 2 hooks

Instructions

1. Thread clothespegs on to the clothesline.
2. Tie a loop at each end of the clothesline and hang it up on hooks screwed into the wall. The line itself should be about level with your head.
3. From the clothespegs, hang photographs that represent, in order, some important events in your child's life. Among the photographs intersperse favourite baby toys and articles of clothing – a T-shirt, first socks and shoes – that help your toddler understand how big she's growing. Add new items as new milestones pass, too.

MY BODY POSTER

This nursery wall decoration can help your toddler learn the printed names for different body parts. And since it's a poster of her, it has built-in appeal.

Ideal Intro Age: 24 months
Age Range: 24 to 36 months

Tools and Materials

☆ Piece of paper at least 1 m (3 ft) wide and slightly longer than your child is tall (you may need to tape together several sheets to make one this size)

☆ Pencil

☆ Crayons or felt-tipped markers

☆ Masking tape

Instructions

1. Lay the paper flat on a hard floor.
2. Help your toddler to lie on her back on the paper. It's best if she's nude or in underwear. Trace around her body with the pencil.
3. Help her to stand up, then retrace the outline with a crayon or marker.
4. Add finishing details: print the names of body parts in large block letters; colour in some hair; add facial features, nipples and belly-button; delineate toes.
5. Hang the poster on the wall with tape, low enough so that the drawn feet touch the floor. This way your child can match herself to her poster.

HINT: Make posters of all the children – Mum and Dad, too. Hang them side by side so you can compare heights.

TO SUM UP

Now that you've helped your child learn who she is, let's look at things she might be. It's time for some fantasy.

the beginnings of fantasy

Older toddlers and pre-schoolers slip quite easily and naturally into make-believe. They're mummies and daddies who care for a brood of assorted dolls, stuffed animals, and other nice and naughty children. They're doctors and nurses, shop assistants and postmen, police officers and firemen, even (as they get older) the superheroes they see on television. In short, they play the roles of any familiar adult who (in their eyes) is wise, powerful and respected. There are ways that you can help this budding fantasy flourish with the props and play suggestions in this chapter.

HOW FANTASY DEVELOPS

The roots of fantasy play lie in the simple imitation games of infancy. At different ages, a baby imitates his parents' facial expressions (for instance, sticking out his tongue), gestures such as waving bye-bye, and actions like giving a kiss or playing pat-a-cake. Sometimes the parent initiates the exchange, other times the baby does. But whatever the imitation, it happens only while both parent and baby are present and actively involved.

A toddler imitates more complicated adult activities. He dusts and sweeps as he has seen his parents do. He pretends to drive a car, or picks up a briefcase and parades around like Daddy. He also acts out little routines with which he's familiar: 'drinking' from an empty cup, 'eating' with an empty spoon, 'washing' his face with a dry cloth, for instance. The difference between these activities and the earlier ones is more than their complexity. He performs them even when a parent is *not* playing with him. Rather than needing someone to copy, he mimics from memory.

Caring for his doll the same way he is cared for by you marks a big shift
in your toddler's fantasy development.

Between 18 and 24 months, he adds a dramatic shift to simple
imitation play. Now he performs familiar routines on dolls and stuffed
animals as well as himself. He washes and feeds his doll, puts it to bed
and hugs it when it 'cries'; that is, he does to the doll what parents
usually do to him. He might take toy characters for rides in a toy car or
bus as he is often taken. In short, he assumes the role of a different
person – usually an adult – and acts out what that familiar character
does. This is the real beginning of the complex and fascinating fantasy
play that's the hallmark of the pre-school years. Soon it grows to
include complicated plots, all kinds of abstract as well as real props,
and other children.

WHY IS IT SO IMPORTANT?

Experts (and parents) used to think that fantasy was at best a waste of time, at worst the sign of a troubled child, maybe even a child possessed. Today we take a lighter view. Fantasy is something that nearly every child enjoys. And most experts agree that it has very positive attributes.

As your child grows, he ventures increasingly beyond the protection of his home and family. In his burgeoning independence he occasionally encounters things that confuse or trouble him — the bullying child next door, the doctor who (although as nice as can be) gives him a painful injection. Even developments at home can be disquieting, especially the arrival of a new baby. Parents, too, come and go according to their schedules, not his whims. It's not surprising that he suffers occasional insecurities.

One way a child deals with these insecurities is through fantasy. He becomes the brave fireman racing to extinguish the flames; he's the daredevil pilot swooping through the skies. On a more familiar note, he's the postman or school bus driver or delivery man, the helpful and respected adult he sees in his own neighbourhood. Or he's the mummy or daddy driving a child (himself!) to the shops or playgroup. These feelings of power and control, fleeting though they may be, help him to feel strong and good about himself.

Naturally, you, his parents, are the most powerful people in your toddler's life, and the ones who exert the most control. When your toddler becomes the parent to a doll or stuffed animal, he enjoys this power, too.

A child works through some bad feelings in fantasy play. He re-creates an unpleasant experience, but changes it to suit his whims. If he's angry in real life at the needle-wielding doctor, in his play he gives the doctor a jab. This makes him feel better. Or perhaps he takes out his momentary jealous feelings about his new baby sister on his uncomplaining teddy bear. This alleviates the need to act out his feelings on his real sister.

These fantasies of power are just that — fantasies. But the good feelings they bring are real, and they make your young child feel much more confident.

Fantasy has correlations with other skills, too. Studies show that children who engage in lots of fantasy play usually perform better than other children in thinking skills tests. They also tend to be better at entertaining themselves, usually have long attention spans, and can say more words.

Fantasy is also linked to that elusive term we call creativity. On the whole, children with active imaginations are more spontaneous, flexible, and able to adapt to new situations than less imaginative children. They also tend to offer more numerous and imaginative ideas in discussions. No one can say whether fantasy leads to this creativity, or whether highly creative children just happen to like fantasy play, but the two are definitely linked.

FOSTERING FANTASY

Although you can't teach a child to be imaginative, you can encourage his natural talent for fantasy, say Dorothy and Jerome Singer. These specialists in play and especially fantasy, believe that, 'While the capacity for fantasy or pretending is inherent in all reasonably normal human beings, the degree to which it is used by children depends to a large degree on whether parents or other adults have fostered it.' You can encourage it by:

○ enlarging your child's world;

○ developing your child's imaginative thinking through a variety of play suggestions;

○ taking part in his fantasy games; and

○ providing toys and props that lend themselves to make-believe play.

Enlarging Your Child's World

○ Read to your toddler. Favourite books will surely become plots he'll later act out. Stories also carry him into fantasy worlds populated by talking cars and engines that can make it over the highest hill (Thomas the Tank Engine) and teddy bears who live like children (especially Paddington).

○ Make up stories. These can be simple tales involving his doll or favourite stuffed animal; stories about the magic bus in front of you as you drive to the market; fables about the family pet. Tailor the length and complexity of these tales to his age and level of comprehension.

o Go on outings. Trips to the zoo, the park, the library, the children's museum, the pet shop, all inspire fantasy re-enactment at home.

Encouraging Imaginative Thinking

o Be imaginative yourself. Look at things differently. Help your toddler to pretend even mundane things are magical. The vacuum cleaner is a dirt-eating dragon, the playground slide an ice-covered mountain, the car a rocket ship ('Everyone into his safety seat for blast-off!'). In the department store, the lift is a time machine, the escalator magic stairs: 'What will we find at the top?'

o Make believe that you are different things. For instance, pretend you're a puppy. Ask your toddler to pet you just as he pets the family pet. Can he be a dog, too? Can he bark like a dog? Or pretend you're the baby and *he's* Daddy.

Encourage imaginative play – suggest and participate in fantasy games.

○ Offer words of encouragement and additional suggestions when your toddler is involved in a fantasy routine. Elaborate on what he's doing, and suggest new directions. If he's playing with a doll, offer something like, 'How nice, you're giving dolly a bath. Did you wash her hair? You'd better wash her hair. . . . Oh, dolly looks so tired now. I think she wants to go to bed. Can you put dolly to bed?' If he's pushing a truck around the floor, ask him: 'What kind of truck is it? What is it carrying? Is it an ice cream van? Can you sell me some ice cream? Where is it going now? Can you make it go to the shop and buy some more ice cream?' Suggest that now it's a fire engine, or a circus lorry. Is your toddler stirring some fantasy concoction in a pot? Suggest he make some soup, some vegetable soup made with bricks, some teddy bear soup, a tennis ball stew. Can he give you a taste?

FANTASY TOYS AND PROPS

Here are some suggested basic and not-so-basic fantasy toys. This list is by no means exhaustive; your toddler turns almost anything into a fantasy prop if it fits in with his scheme or plot.

Dolls and Stuffed Animals

Dolls and stuffed animals are the staples. The mainstay might be a plain plastic baby doll with moulded-on or rooted hair, because it stands up to being washed repeatedly, dunked in a mud puddle, thrown down the stairs, chewed on, covered with food, slammed against the door in a fit of anger. Stuffed animals also get pretty rough treatment at a toddler's hands, so they should be machine washable as well. A simple doll bed (a doll-sized cradle, or perhaps just a shoebox with a folded towel inside) and other similar, plain, sturdy accessories extend fantasy games. And when you join in and play family ('You're the daddy and I'm the mummy and dolly is our baby') the play possibilities are endless.

Plastic Cups, Saucers, Plates

For tea parties with you, brothers and sisters, dolls and stuffed pets, or solitary meals your toddler wants to prepare. NOTE: The elaborate kitchen-type props – cookers, refrigerator, etc. – are usually more appreciated by pre-schoolers than toddlers.

Dolls and stuffed animals are the heart of a younger toddler's make-believe.

Role-playing Props

Since you are your child's absolute number one hero, he'll most often pretend he's Mummy or Daddy. Provide props that he identifies with you: an old wallet or briefcase, a hat, a pair of sunglasses, gloves, slippers. Clothing and personal props like these should be easy for him to put on and take off; when he's a pre-schooler, he'll be more interested in really dressing up in cast-off clothing.

BLUE JEANS BAG

This splendid toddler tote bag sparks lots of fantasy and toddler role playing; it becomes, among other things, a handbag or briefcase that makes a young child feel very grown up indeed. With its roomy centre compartment and several pockets for stuffing things into, it's perfect for holding personal treasures. The button (or snap fastener) and zip let your toddler practise dressing skills. It's just right for games you and your toddler can play, too.

Ideal Intro Age: 24 months
Age Range: 24 to 36 months

Tools and Materials

☆ Pair of old blue jeans or other adult-sized trousers with plenty of pockets and a button or snap fastener

☆ Old cloth belt, or piece of fabric binding about 5 cm (2 in) wide and 60 cm (24 in) long

☆ Scissors

☆ Sewing machine or needle and thread

▶

Instructions

1. Cut both legs off the jeans, about 2.5 cm (1 in) below the crotch; put them aside for other projects.
2. Turn the remaining part of the jeans inside out, sew closed the two leg openings, and turn right-side-out again.
3. To make the two tote bag handles cut the belt or binding into two 30 cm (12 in) pieces.
4. Sew one end of each piece of binding on to the inside of the front waistband; each should be attached about 10 cm (4 in) from the centre closure point.
5. Sew the other end of each strap on to the inside back waistband, opposite the point where attached to the front.

HINTS

○ A sewing machine really simplifies this process. You *can* make it by hand, but it does take longer.
○ Save the legs; one can be used for making the Punching Bag (page 106). The other? Well, use your imagination.

Play Tips

○ Find the Toy: you hide a favourite small toy somewhere in this bag, then ask your toddler to find it.
○ Encourage your toddler to fill the pockets with smaller toys, stuffed animal friends, and the like.
○ Invent little stories you and your toddler can act out. One idea: set an adult-sized chair beside a toddler-sized one. This makes a car in which you two can take a short trip. Make sure he packs everything you need.
○ Have a garden picnic. Your toddler can bring the blanket and non-spillable snacks in his dazzling new bag.
○ Hang the bag over your toddler's bedpost at night. It's great for storing all kinds of otherwise unstorable toys. Plus, a stuffed toy peeking out of the top can keep a protective eye on him while he sleeps.

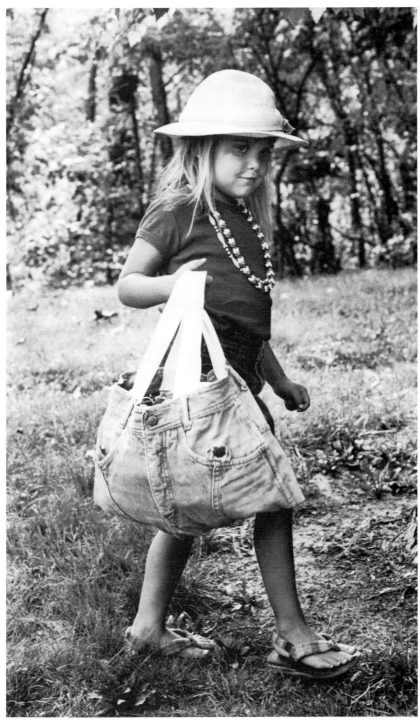

This homemade Blue Jeans Bag makes a young child feel very grown up.

Housekeeping Props

Even daily housekeeping chores seem romantic when you're a toddler; after all, he sees his beloved parents do them. Cut down the handles of an old broom and mop to toddler size. If he demands authenticity, and his wet mopping indoors is too messy, give him his junior mop and a bucket of water and let him clean the porch or garden path.

Cut down the handles of an old broom and mop for your toddler.

Cars and Trucks

Toy vehicles of all kinds are popular because they suit both action and fantasy play. Toddlers love action. They revel in their new abilities to walk and run. They love to make things move, to pull and push and throw toys. They love to watch things move – a car, a lorry, a plane, a dog or cat. Even favourite first words are the names of things that move: *car*, *ball*, *dog*. Toy vehicles certainly fit this interest.

Older toddlers also use toy vehicles in fantasy play. Real cars and lorries and planes, and the people who drive them, are big, exciting things to your toddler. When he acts out scenes with his toy counterparts, he's important, too.

Nearly any type of play vehicle is welcome. Small cars and lorries can also fit into your handbag or pocket for play on outings. Make sure,

For motorway adventures, make a Road Ramp 'n' Tunnel.

though, that the wheels and other tiny pieces are firmly attached; should they come loose, your toddler might put them into his mouth. Larger vehicles offer more dramatic play on the floor. Start your collection now; it'll continue to grow throughout the pre-school years.

Supply some props, too. Small vehicles can fit into a shoebox garage (cut a few tunnel-shaped openings in one of the long sides), larger ones can be housed in a garage made from a cardboard box. Your toddler's indoor slide is a nice mountain for driving up and down. Or try this homemade Road Ramp 'n' Tunnel.

ROAD RAMP 'N' TUNNEL

Ideal Intro Age: 24 months
Age Range: 24 to 36 months

Tools and Materials

☆ Large cardboard box

☆ Ruler

☆ Pencil

☆ Scissors or sharp knife

☆ Felt-tipped markers (optional)

☆ Strong tape (optional)

Instructions

1. Cut off the top flaps of the box.
2. Using the pencil and ruler, draw a diagonal on both sides of the box, as shown.
3. Cut the box in two on the diagonals, and discard the scrap piece.
4. Turn the remaining piece upside down. Cut a tunnel-shaped opening in each supporting side. Cover the cut edges with tape if they're sharp. If you like, decorate the slope to resemble a road.

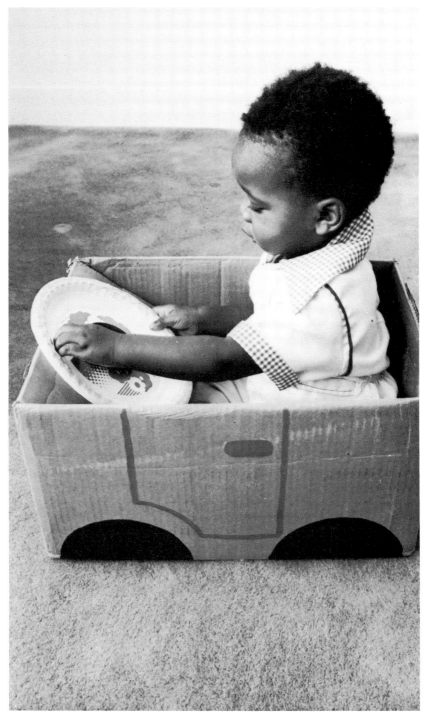

A cosy homemade Box Car inspires countless motor journeys.

BOX CAR

Ideal Intro Age: 24 months
Age Range: 18 to 36 months

Tools and Materials

☆ Cardboard box your child can sit in comfortably

☆ 2 or 3 paper plates, the rigid moulded type with a rim

☆ Large two-pronged paper binder

☆ Large metal washer*

☆ Scissors or sharp knife

☆ Felt-tipped markers

☆ Wrapping or packing tape

Instructions

1. Cut three flaps off the top of the box, leaving one short flap (the steering wheel attaches to this).
2. Tape the paper plates together around their perimeter to make a steering wheel; the double or triple thickness adds durability.
3. Punch holes in the centre of the paper plates and the flap.
4. Thread the washer on to the two-pronged paper binder; insert the binder prongs through the paper plates and the flap, flatten out the prongs on the underside of the flap, and cover the ends with strong tape.
5. Decorate the remainder of the flap to resemble a dashboard (dials, etc.), and the outside of the box to resemble a car: doors on the sides, headlights and brake lights, black half-circles on the bottom for wheels, and so on.

*If you don't have a large metal washer, make one from plastic; cut a large disc from the top of a plastic coffee tin lid and punch a small hole through the centre.

Fantasy Vehicles

Besides making believe with toy vehicles, your toddler likes to drive one himself. The ride-ons he pushed around on at 15 months become the cars, fire engines and ice cream vans he now commandeers throughout your house and garden. See the suggestions on page 101 for tips on choosing appropriate ride-ons.

This homemade car, simple as it may seem compared to the manufactured ones you can buy, has been a favourite of many toddlers I know. Maybe it's because of the simplicity, maybe it's because the sides offer a protected, cosy feeling to the fantasy driver. Since the box cradles and protects, you can push your toddler around the carpeted floor in this toy as fast as you like – he can't fall off or out. The instructions here include a steering wheel that turns. If you're pressed for time or materials, omit this and just decorate the box like a car.

——————— TO SUM UP ———————

Can you remember all the way back – three years ago, is it? – when your child was just a tiny, probably wrinkly and squally newborn, dependent on you for almost everything? And now he's an independent almost-pre-schooler, with boundless skills and a storehouse of knowledge, ready to tackle new challenges. Amazing how much he's changed. And how much you've helped.

appendix

HOMEMADE TOYS: INVALUABLE MATERIALS

These are the standard items to keep on hand. They're listed alphabetically in case you want to refer back to this list when looking at a particular project.

Boxes
Boxes of all kinds and sizes are indispensable for making several of these projects. Get or save:

- Gift boxes, both the flat type that clothing usually comes in and the cube-like type.

- Shoeboxes, and like-sized boxes with lids.

- Larger cartons, scrounged from supermarkets and other shops.

- For giant cartons, check with a shop that sells fridges, washing machines and so on. They may let you have any spare ones.

Clothing, Towels, Linens
One of the easiest ways to make a stuffed toy or pillow is to use existing fabric objects rather than to cut out patterns from flat material. Socks, gloves, T-shirts, old blue jeans, flannels, hand towels and pillowcases can all be transformed into wonderful items in a fraction of the time it would take to make them from scratch.

Elastic
Elastic, about 2.5 cm (1 in) wide, is terrific for hanging toys on the cot or pushchair, or just for dangling toys from your hand, because it stretches and gives when your baby pulls the object.

Fabric
All kinds, all patterns, all textures. If you haven't already, now's the time to start a scrap box. Look for odds and ends and remnants at fabric shops. Save old clothing and bed linen. Always pre-wash fabric that you think might shrink.

Glue
Ordinary all-purpose household glue. The best type is non-toxic, dries clear, and readily washes out of clothing (in case you spill some).

Markers
A set of good felt-tipped markers is a must. Choose the non-toxic washable type, in case your child should get into them.

Mylar
Metallized polyester film (popularly called Mylar) is a thick cellophane-like plastic that's durable, machine washable, dryer safe (at low heat), and noisy when handled. Use Mylar to stuff all or parts of fabric toys; when your baby squeezes the toy, he'll love the delightful crackly sound. Those helium-filled 'mirrored' balloons are usually made of Mylar. Save them!

Newspaper
Great stuffing material for blocks made from cardboard boxes and carrier bags, and even for some fabric toys that won't be washed.

Pictures
Eye-catchers for the young baby, room decorations, books – these and other favourites are all made of pictures. Rather than saving tons of heavily illustrated magazines and catalogues, cut out pictures that might one day be useful and discard the rest of the magazine. Remember that young children love animals, so also look for nature magazines like *National Geographic*. The Sunday colour supplements are good, too. Other sources of pictures:

o Old calendars.

o Posters, especially for room decorations.

o Reproductions of paintings from the art gallery; these usually come in both postcard and small poster size.

o Picture postcards.

o Wrapping paper with bold, bright designs.

Sewing Machine
Not essential, but extremely handy. Some of the fabric toys will probably take longer than thirty minutes to make if you use a needle and thread.

Stanley Knife or Scalpel
This knife consists of a handle with a triangular, very sharp, replaceable blade. A scalpel comes in different sizes, from slender as a pencil to thick as a screwdriver handle. Unbeatable for cutting things out of cardboard.

Stuffing
Polyester fibrefill (sometimes called spun polyester) is sold by the bag at sewing, fabric and

do-it-yourself shops. Get *lots*; you'll be surprised at how much stuffing you can cram into even a small fabric toy. Shredded foam stuffing is also good, but it is heavier and takes longer to dry after washing. You can also stuff small toys with old stockings and tights.

Tape

Handy to have different kinds:

○ Clear adhesive tape for taping pictures into books, etc.

○ Masking tape for taping pictures on walls, etc.

○ Wrapping or packing tape, such as used for wrapping up boxes for shipping. This tape sticks very securely and is very strong. Look for a roll about 3.8–5 cm ($1\frac{1}{2}$–2 in) wide; it's available in stationers and office supply shops. NOTE: This is *not* masking tape; masking tape does not stick nearly as securely.

index